THE BETRAYAL TRAUMA HEALING WORKBOOK

Holistic Healing from Betrayal Trauma, Grief Processing, and 12 Steps for Betrayed Partners of Sexual Addiction

Dr Fai Seyed Aghamiri

Published in Australia by
House of Hope Counselling and Psychotherapy Centre
Unit 10, Mount Lindesay Highway
Browns Plains, QLD, 4118, Australia
houseofhopecounsellingcentre@gmail.com
www.houseofhopecounselling.com.au

First published in Australia by Ultimate World Publishing 2023
Copyright © Dr Fai Seyed 2023

All rights reserved. No part of this publication may be reproduced, stored in a retrieval system, or transmitted, in any form or by any means without the prior written permission of the publisher, nor be otherwise circulated in any form of binding or cover other than that in which it is published and without a similar condition being imposed on the subsequent purchaser

National Library of Australia Cataloguing in Publication entry

 A catalogue record for this book is available from the National Library of Australia

ISBN: 978-0-6457727-1-5 (paperback)
ISBN: 978-0-6457727-2-2 (epub)

Editor: Amanda J Spedding
Printed by Ingram Spark

All care has been taken in the preparation of the information herein, but no responsibility can be accepted by the publisher or author for any damages resulting from the misinterpretation of this work. All details given in this book were current at the time of publication, but are subject to change.

The advice given in this book is based on the experience of the individuals. Professionals should be consulted for individual problems. The author and publisher shall not be responsible for any person with regard to any loss or damage caused directly or indirectly by the information in this book.

"I am leaving you with a gift – peace of mind and heart! And the peace I give isn't fragile like the peace the world gives. So don't be troubled or afraid."

John 14:27 TLB

Dedication

I wish to dedicate this book to The Lord Jesus Christ since He has been the rock on which my life has been built. With unwavering love and limitless faith, God can overcome any betrayal because He is in the business of mending lives and broken hearts. I also dedicate this book to my beloved brother, Alex, whose spiritual awakening and personal growth have been incredibly inspirational. And finally, to all the unique betrayed partners who have been enduring the storms brought on by betrayal and are still choosing to do the hard work that healing demands. You are not victims but valiant victors.

"Lord, have mercy on us. We have put our hope in you. Protect us day by day and save us in times of trouble."

Isaiah 33:2 GNT

Contents

Introduction	ix
1 Your Betrayal Trauma Is Real	1
2 Your Unique Loss And Grief Linked To Betrayal Trauma	33
3 Phases Of Your Betrayal Trauma Linked To Grief	49
4 Anger Phase Of Your Betrayal Trauma Linked To Grief	57
5 Bargaining Phase Of Your Betrayal Trauma Linked To Grief	77
6 Sadness And Depression Phase Of Your Betrayal Trauma Linked To Grief	89
7 Acceptance Phase Of Your Betrayal Trauma Linked To Grief	105
8 Healing From Betrayal Trauma In A Nutshell	133
9 What To Consider Before Ending Your Relationship	171
10 Step Zero And 12 Steps For Processing Your Betrayal Trauma	177
References	242
About the Author	249
Services and Offers	251
Other books by Dr Fai Seyed	253

Dr Fai Seyed Aghamiri

Introduction

What Happened To You?

You are 100% responsible for your own healing even though you had zero responsibility in the trauma caused by the betrayal.

Discovering that your partner has been secretly engaging in unimaginable compulsive behaviours behind your back can be quite traumatic. While some of you might associate your partner's compulsive behaviour with them watching porn and masturbating, others might associate it with greater levels of infidelity and bizarre behaviour. The trauma brought on by this kind of betrayal might occasionally resemble the lingering, dull pain that comes after a sudden punch to the face. However, it is not a complete stranger that attacked you. Instead, it is your intimate partner, who you loved, felt safe with, and never would have expected to act in such a manner. Betrayal trauma experienced by a partner's sexual addiction is more challenging than other forms of trauma.

To separate betrayal trauma from other trauma-related reactions, imagine being invited by your partner to go on a date and participate in an exhilarating skydive. He has a parachute once the plane is in flight, but before you can put yours on, he pushes you out of the aircraft. The fatal blow comes from falling without a parachute and being harmed by the one you perceived as your safe person. In addition to the terrifying free fall and the constant fear about hitting the ground, you are also in excruciating agony and confused by your partner's intentional harm to you—the one who was in charge of ensuring your safety. This multifaceted assault leads to betrayal trauma, a complex emotional roller coaster that can persist for years. If you survive the fall, it becomes challenging to regain your trust in your partner. To be honest, it might be difficult to trust anyone again.

Living in such a reality can be extremely painful once some of the truth (or, if you are lucky, the whole truth) is revealed. You will go through a complicated form of grieving, making it a lifelong journey to deal with the long-term ramifications of such a transgression. Your grief is the intense pain that comes with the countless losses you have suffered due to the betrayal trauma you have experienced. Your grieving is a process without a distinct pattern and very unique to you. This process is your typical emotional reaction to several losses, including losing a trusted partner who betrayed you or other elements of the reality you had grown to believe in and had a great affinity with or affection for. Grief has various aspects in addition to its specific emphasis on the emotional reaction to loss, including intellectual, behavioural, interpersonal, cultural, spiritual, sexual, and philosophical components.

Non-linear phases of grief to be processed frequently include denial, anger, bargaining, depression, and acceptance. Because grief has its own journey and there is no way to entirely escape

Introduction

from suffering, there is no set amount of time for one to grieve after a tragedy of betrayal. Attempting to ignore or avoid grief is just as likely to prolong it and will require more emotional energy. Although the grieving process is generally regarded as a healthy way to cope with loss, occasionally, extended, intense grief can become so crippling that it is recognised as a condition.

Grief processing that acknowledges the hurtful events and situations you have encountered and have been through is the first step in the recovery from betrayal trauma. Initially, you could try to suppress or deny what happened, or you might approach your symptoms in other unhealthy ways, which can seriously harm your relationships and quality of life. This workbook was motivated by my research on the needs of betrayed partners who had discovered their partner's sexual addiction. This book provides various holistic, evidence-based resources to help you manage your grief and emotions. The 12-Steps structure created at the end of the book was developed explicitly for the unique experiences that betrayal trauma causes.

Disclaimer: The use of 'higher power' throughout sections of this book is for those who are non-denominational and have no faith or connection to religiosity. This 'higher power' can be anything you choose: Mother Nature, the Universe, Love…

CHAPTER 1

Your Betrayal Trauma Is Real

*Without suffering, there can be neither
healing nor a need for radical change.*

Have you ever woken up and discovered that everything you believed to be true about your partner and your relationship was a lie? On this first day, the foundation of your existence was unexpectedly demolished. More than merely the discovery or disclosure of the betrayal is emphasised by the partner betrayal-trauma paradigm. It signifies the beginning of a relationship story, the betrayed partner's investment in and commitment to their relationship, the memories and experiences they shared, and the reality of the person and the relationship they were led to believe in with the betrayer.

The nature of betrayal trauma is perplexing and paralysing to the sufferer because this tragic phenomenon demolishes the intimate partner's entire reality system.

A deep bond is ruptured when someone who depends on the intimate attachment for their safety and well-being has been wronged. Betrayal trauma can leave you grieving and tremendously hurting emotionally, physically, spiritually, sexually, and relationally.

The experience of being betrayed by a significant person, such as an intimate partner, parent, caregiver, guardian, or another person who is relied upon for safety, well-being, and protection, distinguishes betrayal trauma significantly from other types of trauma.

After being traumatised by betrayal, you suffer the feeling of going crazy. It pushes your emotional limits, sends you into a tailspin, and draws you in a number of different directions to the point where you are pleading for escape. Your sense of security is shattered, and you lose emotional control as a result. On a psychological level, it is extremely uncomfortable, and you really cannot comprehend how profoundly altering the experience may be unless you have heard the narratives or seen the reactions of others who have been through it. As if that were not enough, your brain begins to behave differently when betrayal occurs. Hypervigilance, agitation, anxiety, and a sense of always being on alert stem from the fear-centre/trauma-brain becoming active and staying activated. This has an impact on your ability to manage your emotions, remain composed, think clearly, and reason. When your fear centre takes over your every-day functioning, everything feels difficult, your mind will not stop racing, your emotions feel out of control, and your coping systems are stretched to the limit. This is a betrayal-trauma experience that is dynamic, multifaceted, and multidimensional.

The body's Autonomic Nervous System (ANS) goes into overdrive and prepares for danger in less than a millisecond after trauma. When the body detects danger, it sends messages throughout the body that cause the release of adrenaline, cortisol, and other stress hormones to rise. This primes the body to defend itself, flee, or, if none of these options are viable, to shut down. The body is built to be able to react to stress in this way before calming down and regaining a balanced state of being that is alert but relaxed. Consider this as an emergency brake system that is there for you when you need it but is not meant to be utilised constantly.

Betrayal trauma can occur in conjunction with instances of gaslighting and other deceitful behaviour and can result in severe anxiety and despondence. How much trauma is caused determines the impact. Your level of trauma may not be comparable to other trauma experiences when you discover that your intimate partner has been acting out sexually with themselves and/or with others because this is a distinct type of trauma.

When infidelity linked to sex addiction is discovered or revealed, betrayed partners experience a persistent emotional state of threat and dread. After the first indication of betrayal, the body will immediately activate its threat-response mechanism. Sadly, partners usually deal with a never-ending stream of discoveries that constantly set off the brain's alarm system, causing it to flare up and prepare to confront, escape, or shut down. Many betrayed partners claim they have had a feeling of their system exploding into disarray just when they are beginning to feel calm and collected. In other words, the body's threat-response mechanism continues to be engaged in response to the ongoing discoveries of betrayal and the very real fear of impending betrayals. Instead of acting as an emergency brake system, this degree of high activity becomes chronic. Because of this, betrayed partners commonly find themselves trying to balance their every-day responsibilities while their threat system is running full steam ahead. They are essentially dealing with the initial trauma as well as the constant worry about experiencing more trauma in the future.

Long before any discovery or disclosure, betrayed victims may suffer from physical and mental distress. Even if the betrayed partner is not yet aware of the actual betrayal, the ongoing feeling that their partner is not truly intimate, open, or present, that something is off, or the relationship is in difficulty, can be distressing. Additionally, the betrayal-trauma hypothesis states that a person is more likely to be "unaware" or "blind" to a betrayal the more significant they perceive a person (such as an intimate partner) or institution to be in their life. The betrayed partners themselves, as well as outside observers, frequently ask, "How could I not detect what was going on?" or "How could they not perceive what was happening?"

The phenomena of betrayal-trauma blindness might provide some insight into why someone might continue to engage with a sex-addict partner despite their recurrent relapses or remain in a narcissistic and/or abusive relationship.

Trauma bonding and hysterical hypersexuality

Your brain is fired up and malfunctioning as a result of the revelations. It does not know what to do. You want either to push the person who injured you away or draw them closer – or both. In my research on betrayed partners, I discovered that they were caught in a pendulum swing between dread of being with the addicted partner and a desire for intimacy and re-attachment with them. The betrayed partner increases their sexual engagement with the offender during this brief post-betrayal phase.

Usually, you may realise that your feelings for your partner fluctuate from "I can't bear to look at him/her" and "I want him/her to stay with me" and engaging sexually with them.

This is a trauma response, so you should not feel bad about it, just be mindful that you need to discuss and process this occurrence with your therapist.

Why? After experiencing betrayal, which is a terrible and challenging event, you could feel devastated, deceived, angry, and deeply traumatised. This painful and baffling experience may make you feel confused, vulnerable, and alone. It may cause you to lose trust in yourself and other people. You probably constantly ask your partner, "How could you lie so much? Why did you cheat on me? How did you maintain your façade for such a long time? If you really do love me the way you say you do, how could you have injured me in this way?"

The betrayed partners are understandably desperate and demand answers. They need explanations that will end their pain and provide a safer and more confident future. Without it, there is still uncertainty and a very real possibility of additional betrayals. To put it simply, the deceived is asking, "How can you guarantee you won't betray me again if we don't know why you did this?"

In reality, following years of research of this topic and interaction with those who have betrayed their partners, the only conclusion I can come to is that they most certainly do not have a satisfactory response. I wish I could assure you that there is one compelling answer to at least one of these questions that your broken heart would receive. It is attempting to make sense of a senseless situation. Regardless of how unfair or cruel it may sound, I encourage you—the betrayed—to try to understand the intellectual justifications for their nonsensical actions. Of course, you should do this when you are emotionally ready.

When exploring the psychological roots of what drives someone to engage in compulsive sexual behaviours, it is critical to keep in mind that there is rarely a simple cause-and-effect finding that explains them. The truth is that adverse childhood experiences—sexual, physical, and/or psychological trauma—have a significant impact on how individuals, including your partner, believe in and perceive themselves.

Oftentimes, these negative self-perceptions and/or mistrust of others follow children into adulthood and into their intimate relationships. Given that childhood trauma has been demonstrated to have such a profoundly negative impact on coping and interpersonal interactions, it makes sense that some people—like your partner—who have gone through traumatic events as children may be more susceptible to numerous mental health conditions, covert acting-out behaviours, intimacy dysfunction and infidelity.

I can clearly hear you saying, "BS! I went through bigger trauma and I didn't become a cheater and liar." Unquestionably, you are correct. No matter what life throws at one, there are always plenty of other options to consider rather than committing to deceit or infidelity, so I am not trying to minimise the betrayal or the terrible decisions that turned your entire world upside down. However, because trauma and trauma processing are highly subjective (individual) experiences, not everyone will react or perceive them in the same way. The unfortunate truth is that your unfaithful partner and others, in general, do not share your sense of morality and values either.

The aftermath of betrayal trauma includes the possibility of the betrayed spouse's unhealed emotional wounds resurfacing. This may indicate that triggers may become more intense and that long-held but deeply buried feelings of rejection, abandonment, and mistrust will intensify and impede healing. Furthermore, the brain releases dopamine and oxytocin to produce feelings of connection and satisfaction when there is a sense of relational belonging and trust. Betrayal can cause these feel-good hormones to be disrupted as a result of abandonment or rejection. In fact, a lot of additional factors could harm the betrayed brain's chemistry in the short- or long-term.

I can hear you saying, "Gee, do I have to face my own trauma that I thought I had released in addition to the devastation my addicted partner has created?" Unfortunately, the answer is yes. Life, in its kindness and wisdom, enables us to temporarily bury some of our past wounds because we have not been equipped, or mature enough to address them. It is also common to experience trepidation and significant resistance when old hurts have been triggered. However, one advantage of going through difficult periods in life is that these tragic occurrences periodically compel us to face the trauma we have been carrying around but not dealing with. Make the decision to let your heart heal because nothing your partner has done has been of your making or choosing. Decide to become a victor instead of continuing to be a victim; take charge of your own recovery, and focus on your well-being. You are valuable and unique.

Note that following the discovery or disclosure of betrayal, it is common that you are doubting practically everyone and everything. Because it is too much to keep others close any longer, you are pushing people away. There are some you simply do not want to bring into your personal hell. As you move through the ashes, you let some people in but have to keep others out. That is ok. The only person who will ever really understand what it is like to live with a sex addict, is you, the betrayed partner. Even when someone is trying very hard to recover from addiction, not everyone chooses to remain with them. Your decisions are valid, unique to you, and your experiences and pain are also valid. And that's perfectly alright.

Trying to find a balance between every-day pressure and expectations, and the uncertainty of an addict's long-term recovery is stressful. In a similar vein, I frequently hear the betrayed partners doubting their own decisions and new realities. I commonly hear betrayed partners ask, "What does it mean to choose to live with a sex addict?"

Do you contemplate if you are naive, co-dependent, or just plain stupid?

Do you constantly worry that your life will collapse at some point?

Do you struggle to reconcile the parts of your life with the addict that were real and the parts that were not? As a result, your trauma-brain convinces you to succumb to the notion that it was all a big lie.

Undoubtedly, it is incredibly distressing and traumatising for a partner to discover they have been living together and having an intimate relationship with someone who has violated their consent or choices regarding the addict's compulsive sexual behaviour.

Recovering from living with a sex addict and the betrayal trauma brought on by their activities will undoubtedly be one of your toughest challenges. The worst day in a partner's life is unquestionably discovery day. On this day, you first learned about his or her secret life. It was on this day when your life, as you previously knew it, was forever altered.

Whether as the betrayed partner you choose to quit the relationship or not, you will spend a lot of time reflecting during this stage. "Why? Why me? How were they able to? How did they manage?

When did it begin? Imagine if... Now what?" My research on betrayed partners led me to the conclusion that the betrayed partner will have a different and, at times, more bleak outlook on life. They have profound wounds that, despite time, will never completely heal. The betrayed partners are changed forever, not by their own free will but because it was chosen for them.

The betrayed partner and the addict must both allow the healing process time while purposefully carrying out the necessary individual and (if they are still together) relational work. Because it takes the brain at least three to five years to rewire, be it the addict in recovery or their traumatised partner.

Healing requires both hard labour and, most crucially, consistency. While reading this book, you may come across a number of confronting issues, some of which may cause you resistance and unwillingness to complete. Dealing with these difficult issues immediately rather than delaying them may be beneficial for you. Betrayed partners who actively work on healing and are dedicated to it are more likely to make progress than those who put it off and whine about lack of progress and being stuck. Because your healing is solely your responsibility and is only achievable if you put in the necessary work, the effectiveness of this workbook or any other resource is totally dependent on the level of effort you put into it. This is consistent with the notion that in most areas of life, you get back precisely what you put in. Therefore, try to dedicate at least 20 to 30 minutes a day to concentrate on your own intentional healing.

In addition to working on your own healing, you must educate yourself about the true nature of sexual addiction and its presenting characteristics. This will lessen the likelihood of engaging in rescuing behaviours or falling prey to the addict's manipulation. For instance, the majority of sex addicts engage what I refer to as **"deceptive**

reality" in their daily lives, prior to active recovery, and to a lesser extent throughout ongoing recovery. This suggests that even if they never follow through on a statement, if they say it insistently and honestly enough, it will seem real to them at the time. This results from years of self-deception in order to deceive others.

But this pattern shows that the behaviour and execution of the promised action do not need to occur for it to be true in the addict's perception. The sex addict believes what they say as they are saying it, so even if they do not follow through on their "promise", it is enough in their eyes. When someone claims they want to change but does not participate in relational and individual recovery work, does not go to meetings, or does not make calls, their behaviour speaks for itself. If you let sincere, deceptive reality trick you, do not blame the addict. However, it is crucial to remember that you have no control over your partner's addiction or recovery, and that they can only change things if they so choose. But you have complete control over knowing about this mind-altering condition, execution of your boundaries, and consequences.

Should you decide to continue an intimate relationship with an addict in recovery, do not disregard the red flags. Doing so could only result in more misery and suffering (if they are not wholeheartedly committed to changing, because some people may never be able to break unhealthy habits). To determine whether your addicted partner is genuinely **doing recovery** or is merely **in recovery**, you must cultivate mindful trust based on believing their behaviour.

Acting enabling, gullible, domineering, or intimidatingly while attempting to steer their recovery bus is not healthy nor helpful. Additionally, some addicts rapidly pick up on what their betrayed partners want to hear and have learned there are no consequences for disregarding boundaries. These people will then become "I'm going to" but are truly never the "going to" sort of people. To put it another way, even they may believe that a proclamation or promise they make in the moment is true, but they will never carry out the activity they have pledged.

As the betrayed spouse, you must therefore emphasise the significance of believing behaviour and the alignment of your partner's actions and words instead of their deceptive reality-making.

You must not let the possibility of a relapse keep you from focusing on your own healing. As previously mentioned, you are powerless over your addicted partner's changes. But the boundaries and consequences you establish for your own safety, partner's addiction, tolerance of their dysfunctional behaviour, evidence for their recovery and your commitment to your healing are entirely up to you. You alone bear full responsibility for them.

It is a bitter truth you need to simultaneously complete your own work while juggling trauma symptoms, triggers, and opposing chatter in your head. One voice tells you that you are a fool for staying, and the other insists that everyone deserves a second chance, especially if your partner is repentant and not repeating their mistake. Give yourself grace and time knowing that you do not need to make a permanent decision based on temporary, trauma-induced emotions. Sometimes, the wisest course of action is to take no action because once you've healed sufficiently, you'll be able to make much more sensible decisions.

The amount of deliberate work you put forth will determine how well you recover.

Some Of The Signs And Symptoms Of Betrayal Trauma

- Intrusive thoughts and images.
- Avoidance behaviours and a persistent sense of dread.
- Flashbacks or nightmares.
- Hypervigilance; being on the lookout for potential hazards all the time.
- Anger or irritability.
- Sleep difficulties.
- Social isolation.
- Emotional numbness.
- Panic attacks.
- Suicidal thoughts.
- Self-harm behaviours.
- Over or undereating.
- Excessive drinking or screen time.
- Autoimmune illness.
- Headaches or migraines.
- Fatigue.
- Lack of focus.
- Depression.
- Severe anxiety.
- Shame, guilt, and self-blame.
- Low self-esteem and self-worth.
- Negative self-beliefs and others, such as "I am not good enough", "Everyone is a liar" or "I can't trust myself or others".

- Sudden mood swings.
- Emotional dysregulation.
- Having trouble sustaining relationships or letting people get close.
- Intimacy dysfunctions.
- Lack of decision making.
- Lack of self-care.
- Memory problems (e.g. forgetfulness, memory distortion, factually incorrect memories).
- More.

Practical steps toward healing

Continuous therapy (i.e. individual and relational), as well as a confirmed therapeutic disclosure if you choose to remain in your relationship. Therapy is meant to be a safe place where you may speak openly about your most intimate thoughts and feelings without worrying about being judged or retaliated against. Your therapist is there to listen to you with an open mind, to help you create coping mechanisms, to help you see things from different perspectives, and to help you move on in a healthy manner.

Educate yourself regarding the nature of sexual addiction. Partners who have been betrayed discover that the betrayer is a secretly-entitled, destructive person. The betrayed partner's recovery depends on receiving information about the circumstances that led to the betrayer's decisions and deception. It is difficult to comprehend that individuals who battle sex addiction act out sexually with themselves or others while still loving their partner (in the way they perceive love). Partners who have been betrayed struggle to learn and believe that addiction is a separation of the self. Nevertheless, the betrayer's heinous actions are still in no way justified or vindicated by this.

Set clear boundaries. Setting clear boundaries and consequences for boundary violations are terrific techniques to make yourself and your relationship safe.

Interoception is the capacity you have to comprehend your own emotional sensations. Interoception means sensing internal signals from your body. Our body's physical experiences and emotions are related. For instance, you might have butterflies in your stomach when you are nervous, or you might feel outraged when someone violates your boundaries. Your muscles will tense up, your heart rate will increase, and you will begin to feel warm. These feelings are recognised by interoception. Interoception and our emotional system are linked. It has been demonstrated that our capacity to recognise and self-regulate our emotional states is directly correlated with our capacity to understand our own physical cues. For instance, you would know to calm down and take a few deep breaths if you could feel yourself becoming hot from rage. Our capacity to discern our own physical signals and emotional states has a direct bearing on our capacity to discern the physical and emotional states of others. Following severe traumatic events, interoception plays a critical role in the regulation of the nervous system. Experiencing trauma can cause you to deactivate your internal senses, or interoception, in order to stay vigilant and survive in your environment. You did not need to be aware of your emotions, hunger, thirst, or even your heartbeat or breathing to survive. In reality, those internal feelings and emotions may have caused greater relational harm, so you rapidly learnt to suppress them. As a result, like a majority of trauma survivors, you lost bodily connection and awareness. Interoception training, however, can aid in their recovery. Interoception is a technique for acknowledging your emotions, keeping an eye on oneself and bodily sensations so that you can increase your sense of pleasure, lessen your feelings of pain, and make sure you have the resources you need at any given time.

Ways to improve interoception:

- Journaling your feelings and identify your physical sensations.
- Notice the connection of your mind and body.
- Mindfulness meditation practices.
- Yoga.
- Deep-breathing exercises.

Acknowledge instead of avoid. The first step to actively attempting to address the betrayal trauma is accepting that you have been betrayed. Those who suffer from betrayal blindness frequently fail to recognise their own trauma, since doing so can be too painful and overwhelming. Recognising trauma from betrayal gives you the ability to take charge of your healing. You might be able to use the pain and anguish of betrayal as a springboard for personal development and, if required, put safety precautions in place to avert further hurt. Once you can accept what has happened, you may start looking for appropriate coping mechanisms to help you get through the healing process.

Recognise the triggers and actively use trigger-management resources. Triggers are any noises, images, scents, or feelings that bring back painful experiences. Depending on your individual background, betrayal-trauma triggers can take many different shapes.

Steps In Your Trigger Management:

- Notice you are having a trigger.
- Name it.
- Externalise it by reminding yourself your trauma-brain is activated and the trigger appears to be a real threat. Look for facts that you are safe.
- Use some (or all) of these tools to manage your trigger:
  - Put a rubber band around your wrist and snap it a few times.
  - Take some slow, deep breaths.
  - Ground yourself through naming three things you see, three things you can smell, three things you can touch and describe their texture, three things you can hear.
  - Drink something mindfully.
- Engage in regular self-care routines such as:
  - Journal about your triggers and how they make you feel emotionally and physically.
  - Engage in some physical activity.
  - Listen to music.
  - Go for a walk.
  - Play with a pet.
  - Take a bath.
  - Meditate.
  - Paint.
  - Reach out and connect with a safe person.
  - Pray, read spiritual or faith-based scripture.

Identifying and accepting your emotions. Practise sitting in your emotions and accepting them instead of escaping them through excessive work, screen time or other preoccupations. An essential component of healing from betrayal trauma is accepting unpleasant emotions. Recognise your emotions as they arise and try to address them head-on. In order to move past them and take control of your life, name your feelings without judgement or blame. Acceptance is the understanding that difficult feelings will come and go as a necessary component of the healing process, not that you agree with your thoughts, feelings or the circumstance. Naming your emotions may help you better understand and control them. Additionally, it gives you the impression that you are in control of your emotions rather than letting them control you. Some emotions might be too strong to understand; instead of trying to make sense of them, try to "feel" your way through them. You can achieve this by becoming aware of your bodily experiences and paying attention to your body's cues. For the time being, you might find that identifying the bodily sensations you are having, such as "I have heart palpitations" or "My heart is racing" or "My chest feels tight and it is difficult to breathe", is sufficient.

Look after your mind and body. Achieving and maintaining positive mental and physical health are correlated. Eating healthily and scheduling time for self-care are both parts of nurturing your body. The body and mind are closely intertwined even if they appear to be separate. You take care of yourself by establishing a solid foundation for your mental health and physical well-being and by consistently meeting your body's nutritional and physical activities. Rest and hydrate as you need.

Here are ways to take care of your body:

- Frequently consume water.
- Choose healthy meals that are high in vegetables.
- To improve your mental health, find a form of exercise you enjoy.
- Develop healthy sleep patterns.
- Engage in self-care.
- Get a medical check.

If you have experienced betrayal related to a sexual addiction, this becomes even more crucial. When infidelity or sex addiction are exposed or discovered, it is rare for all the information and facts to be given. Even though it could be frightening to ponder the possibility of having an STD or STI, speak with a doctor to be sure.

Practise mindfulness and gratitude. Gaining greater awareness of the present moment as it is felt in our body is the goal of mindfulness. It is not about attempting to modify your thoughts or empty your head. It is about observing and acting compassionately rather than negatively. Practise gratitude every day by reminding yourself of your blessings. Be precise. At night, note them down or repeat them again in your head.

Create a safe space to self-regulate. Establish a safe space where you can retreat and ground yourself. This is a pleasant and comfortable location where you can withdraw mentally or physically when times are difficult. Having a few safe spaces, such as a room or particular area in the home or nearby—a garden, beach, a mountain, or a park—is a good idea. In this space, practise breathing deeply. Your breathing becomes shallower and shorter when you are dysregulated and under stress, which actually makes you feel more disturbed or anxious. Your nervous system is reset to a calmer state when you breathe slower and deeper from your belly, which might help you relax when you are overwhelmed or overstimulated.

Share your experience with safe people and form healthy relationships. You can process your thoughts and feelings in a safe environment by sharing your experiences with sympathetic and encouraging others. This could be your therapist, a member of your family, a friend, or a support group who share similar experiences. You need the help of people to avoid becoming caught in harmful thought or behaviour patterns that will only make your problems worse, so stay connected and try not to self-isolate. Healing is only possible within the support and comfort of a community of safe people. It is tremendously therapeutic and helpful to share and hear other people's narratives. When you hear those experiences, you gain knowledge from them and discover how they cope and heal. Even while it could occasionally seem too difficult, this can inspire you to take the necessary actions for your own healing. At some point, the people you love will let you down. You can essentially feel free to be who you are in a safe relationship, which is what separates a healthy relationship from a toxic one. Any mistakes or hurt feelings can be discussed with the other person. When the dialogue is over, you feel heard and understood. You may need to include this in your therapy goals if you have trouble building healthy relationships in your life and avoid people all the time.

Invest in your own personal development. As soon as you begin the process of healing from the trauma of betrayal and put your newly acquired abilities into practise, you will start to notice new growth in your life. This growth is inescapably sustainable. The process of growth that happens after a trauma of betrayal is referred to as "post-traumatic growth". However, it does not happen naturally. It calls for intentional and ongoing commitment and investment in yourself.

QUESTIONS

How, and by whom have you been betrayed?_____
_____
_____
_____
_____
_____

What facets of your life have been affected by this betrayal? Be detailed._____
_____
_____
_____
_____

What did the betrayal mean? _____
_____
_____
_____
_____
_____

What symptoms did you experience following betrayal trauma?

_____

_____

_____

_____

_____

What does self-care mean to you? _____

_____

_____

_____

_____

_____

How has the past betrayal prevented you from getting what you want in life? _____

_____

_____

_____

_____

What does your inner voice say about you and the reasons for the betrayal?_____

_____

_____

_____

_____

Did you engage in trauma bonding or hysterical hypersexuality after learning about your partner's sexual behaviour?_____

_____

_____

_____

_____

What did it mean to you to engage in hysterical hypersexual behaviour with your addicted partner? How did you feel afterward?

_____

_____

_____

_____

Based on facts and not feelings, how true is your negative inner voice? Explain. _____

_____

_____

_____

_____

What does your positive inner voice say about you and the reasons for the betrayal? _____

_____

_____

_____

_____

Based on facts and not feelings, how true is your positive inner voice? Explain. _____

_____

_____

_____

_____

_____

Based on facts, did you cause the betrayal? Explain.

What could you have done to prevent the betrayal?

Can you cure the betrayal or even the one who betrayed you? Explain.

If you were to no longer hold on to betrayal, what new opportunities would come into your life? _____

_____

_____

_____

_____

What triggers did you experience earlier versus now? _____

_____

_____

_____

_____

_____

What tools do you employ for trigger management? Which one(s) do you believe to be the most effective? _____

_____

_____

_____

_____

_____

What negative thoughts and beliefs do you hold regarding your partner and yourself?_____

_____

_____

_____

_____

_____

_____

Do you ever feel alone in life? Explain._____

_____

_____

_____

_____

_____

How can you deal with the loneliness that the trauma of betrayal has given you?_____

_____

_____

_____

_____

How do you remain composed when conversing with others or your partner? _____

_____

_____

_____

_____

_____

How do you listen to your partner and others' opinions without judgement? _____

_____

_____

_____

_____

During interactions with your partner and others, how do you address any anger, impatience, or defensiveness in yourself? ____

_____

_____

_____

_____

_____

How do you show and communicate empathy to others and/or to your partner?_____

_____

_____

_____

_____

_____

What encouraging words may you say to yourself to help you remember your strength?_____

_____

_____

_____

_____

_____

Give an example of a scenario with your partner in which you felt traumatised again? _____

_____

_____

_____

_____

_____

In order to avoid re-traumatisation or triggers, what could you do differently the next time in a similar scenario? What would you do to empower yourself? _____

_____

_____

_____

_____

I like who I am because: _____

_____

_____

_____

_____

I don't like these aspects of myself: _____

_____

_____

_____

and need to address them by: _____

_____

_____

_____

I am pleased with myself because: _____
_____
_____
_____
_____

Others think I'm fantastic at these five areas: _____
_____
_____
_____
_____

I'm very proud of myself for: _____
_____
_____
_____
_____

My immediate and long-term goals are: _____
_____
_____
_____
_____

What were five things today that you found peaceful? _____

_____
_____
_____
_____

What were the five minor victories you had today? _____

_____
_____
_____
_____

Who/what are the five special things and individuals who give you confidence in yourself? _____

_____
_____
_____
_____

I'm grateful for the following five things or persons, because: __

_____
_____
_____
_____

What self-care practices do you require and want to introduce?

_____
_____
_____
_____
_____

How do you intentionally create space and time for my self-regulation?

_____
_____
_____
_____
_____

How do you define self-care? What routines do you follow? ___

_____
_____
_____
_____
_____

CHAPTER 2

Your Unique Loss And Grief Linked To Betrayal Trauma

*Betrayal is not grieving a single loss.
In reality, there is a long list of losses.*

Once you learn of your partner's sexual addiction, it is common to feel as though your emotional equilibrium is slipping. Strong emotional reactions, the loss of a familiar life, and the experience of loss and grief can all happen swiftly and unexpectedly. Tears, self-doubt, melancholy, indignation, worry, and conflicting feelings are examples of strong emotional reactions as well as wanting to stay in the relationship one minute but wanting to leave it the next. It is critical to understand that, despite being excruciatingly painful, your emotional experiences are a typical response to traumatic occurrences. One of the most frequent and underappreciated reactions to betrayal is grief. Even if you and your partner are able to patch things up, your relationship will not be the same. Knowing that your feelings are a manifestation of trauma reactions and grief may enable you to find your emotional needs and seek resources to meet them.

Tame your inner critic

Discovering your spouse has deceived you may cause pre-existing or new self-esteem problems to worsen. The thought that you are to blame for your partner's behaviours because you are weak in some way is a type of self-attack that has no place in your recovery. Self-blame can either be obvious or subtle. While some may now consider themselves as "fools" for being ignorant of the concealed behaviours, others may hold themselves accountable for any inadequacies they believe contributed to the betrayal. The first and most important step in quieting this poisonous voice is awareness. Construct self-statements and affirmations to counter any feelings of guilt or low self-esteem. Do not worry if you do not truly believe these thoughts at first when you are expressing them. The objective is to provide a counterbalanced mindset to stop self-blame and self-esteem issues from getting out of hand.

Grief is a normal emotion. Extreme tragedy can bring about significant change because your mind, body and spirit primarily use grief to turn trauma and suffering into harmony and, eventually, acceptance. However, grieving is a process that many people find difficult, and some may even attempt to avoid it by fleeing from it. You can try to ignore it, be afraid of it, or even escape it instead of allowing it to be transformed. The problem is that all of these strategies are harmful and ineffective, which can only result in further detrimental effects.

While people frequently associate grief with the aftermath of a death, grief is actually the way one processes and copes with loss. Many of the same things experienced by someone who has lost a loved one will also happen to you. However, betrayal grief may appear and feel different because the other person is still alive, but your previous relationship with them and your conception of who you thought they were, have changed, if not been completely destroyed. This may actually make processing emotions and discovering new meaning even more difficult than with grieving after a death because it is a less concrete and more ambiguous loss. Moreover, your loss is much more complicated in many respects since you can have little to no support and feel like you have to carry this secret, possible judgement, stigma, and the humiliation. Your specific type of grief falls under the socially "unrecognisable" or "less evident" grief category and is therefore more challenging to endure.

Finding safe people who can help you navigate your grief and losses, however, is crucial. Your capacity to move on from your partner's betrayal rests on your capacity to accept the losses it has caused you and to give yourself permission to grieve. This holds true whether or not there is a reconciliation. Grief brought on by the trauma of betrayal is complex and compels you to acknowledge numerous severe losses.

A Betrayed Partner May Grieve The Following Losses:

- Loss of relational trust.
- Loss of emotional, sexual, financial, spiritual safety.
- Loss of hope/dreams.
- Loss of faith in self, others and God/higher power.
- Loss of intimacy and affection.
- Loss of self-esteem.
- Loss of trust in self and others.
- Loss of concept of what commitment in a relationship entails.

Good grief practice

Grief is the only way to deal with the loss and suffering caused by betrayal.

Your grief does not follow a schedule. Additionally, how you express and handle grief is influenced by cultural and contextual factors. Furthermore, numerous factors, including your fundamental personality and sexual identity, social interactions, the seriousness of the loss, cultural conventions, and whether you are an emotional or intellectual being, affect how and for how long you grieve. These factors include prior loss experiences, the family structure, and early portrayals of grief. Your response to the losses caused by betrayal will depend on how you have previously dealt with other losses. Some people openly and brazenly cry when they are grieving. Others reserve their tears for exclusive, closed-door moments. Many use art or other creative work to convey their pain. They are not attempting to conceal their feelings; rather, they are using their actions as a way to purposefully process them. Others could use anger to convey it.

Although you may not grieve as others do, do not judge yourself. Do not avoid processing your pain because that will only prolong your healing. It is important to realise there are no sequential stages of grief. The previous phase is not completed before moving on to the next. There are five stages of grief, according to Elizabeth Kübler. Despite the fact there is no prescribed period of time or method for grieving, I like to emphasise the significance of making a conscious effort to create time and space to acknowledge your grief, and to allow yourself to grieve in order to prevent remaining stuck in grief. In fact, the ability to grieve the loss properly makes a significant difference in whether someone moves on with a new life after experiencing betrayal.

What should you do if a long period has passed since the betrayal and you are still within grief?

After being betrayed, it is common to experience prolonged hurt. Give yourself time to grieve the loss if you find it difficult to go on after the betrayal. You run the risk of causing more harm and disconnectedness if you try to ignore or run away from your loss. Unattended and untransformed grief and pain may surface in surprising but harmful ways. It is generally presented as anger, resentment and contempt. Unresolved grief-induced trauma eventually turns toxic, manifesting as despair, isolation, and distrust in the people around you. Playing the victim while blaming self-preservation for your lack of healing and trying to weaponise your pain to prove everyone else wrong will only make things worse and hurt you more. Therefore, if your mourning lasts a long time, you should think about seeing a therapist because it will be difficult for you to create a new purpose in life or maintain a healthy lifestyle. This will help you process your grief and betrayal and begin moving on.

How To Grieve And How To Honour Your Grief

- Be kind and gentle to yourself and acknowledge that facing significant fears are essential steps in overcoming your grief.

- Acknowledge and accept the reality of the loss. You may tell yourself, "It's bloody hard and unjust, but it is what it is." After a loss, shock, numbness, and disbelief are typically experienced. People frequently and mistakenly believe that shock indicates bravery, yet shock actually indicates the opposite. The emotions that come to the surface when shock and numbness wear off could come as a surprise tsunami to the person.

- While acknowledging and honouring your suffering when it does emerge, and the fact that it takes time for the pain to completely disappear, find solace in the times when you are not in excruciating pain.

- While you are grieving, seek professional support. Awareness gives you the ability to control your emotions and sit in them appropriately.

- As your journey progresses, finding a safe person or a safe group is undoubtedly one of your best resources.

- Consciously work your way through the stages of grief. Melancholy, anxiety, righteous anger, hopelessness, alienation, shame, remorse, and even a feeling of insanity or mental confusion are examples of normal emotions. After grief sets in, there is frequently a back-and-forth movement between acute betrayal feelings and intervals when the person returns to shock and numbness. Your brain uses this strategy to shield you from multiple painful feelings at once.

*Unattended grief simply leads to further grief
—for oneself and for others.*

Since grieving is a continuous process, compassion and mindfulness are needed at all times. The effects of the grieving process includes thoughts, feelings, and behaviours. Identify the various ways in which the betrayal and your grief are present in your thinking. Find out what each thought makes you feel (pay attention to your bodily sensations too). In order to create emotional regulation when grieving after a betrayal, it is crucial to pay attention to the feelings that emerge and understand their significance. It could feel more convenient in the time to push aside or dismiss uncomfortable feelings. However, repressing feelings rather than allowing oneself to experience and process them leads to only transient comfort. Eventually, suppressed feelings will come back or manifest themselves in new destructive ways. Describe in detail the actions that each feeling causes you to take. The only way to navigate the layers of your pain, hold space for yourself, finding healthy coping mechanisms, and promote understanding and validation of your own experiences is to acknowledge and accept your unique way of grieving.

QUESTIONS

The thoughts of Betrayal:

Thoughts about the injustice of it are:_____

_____

_____

_____

_____

_____

_____

_____

Thoughts concerning what you ought to have said or done differently:_____

_____

_____

_____

_____

_____

_____

_____

Your Unique Loss And Grief Linked To Betrayal Trauma

Your feelings attached to the thoughts of Betrayal:
- Fear
- Anger
- Hatred

_____
_____
_____

Based on the feelings connected to the betrayal, how did you act?
- Utilise distraction tactics to avoid
- Self-isolation

_____
_____
_____

Write down all of your thoughts below:_____
_____
_____
_____
_____
_____
_____
_____

Write down all of your feelings below:_____

_____
_____
_____
_____
_____
_____
_____
_____
_____

Write down all your actions based on your feelings:_____

_____
_____
_____
_____
_____
_____
_____
_____
_____

Your Unique Loss And Grief Linked To Betrayal Trauma

What losses are you grieving? Explain each.

___

Do you have any previous grief? Is this comparable or different?

Who did you share your grief story with? _____
_____
_____
_____
_____
_____

What unfavourable experiences did you encounter while wanting to share your grief with others? _____
_____
_____
_____
_____
_____

What kind of support have you had in coping with your loss and grief? _____
_____
_____
_____
_____
_____

Did you feel like you had to hide your grief or could you express it openly? _____

_____
_____
_____
_____
_____
_____

Was the whole story of your relationship a lie? _____

_____
_____
_____
_____
_____
_____

Which emotions are currently making you feel the most uncomfortable? _____

_____
_____
_____
_____
_____
_____

If you have not already, what would you say to your loved ones about your way of grieving? _____

_____

_____

_____

_____

Have you given yourself permission to occasionally enjoy life, or is your grief still controlling you?_____

_____

_____

_____

_____

When you are experiencing grief overload, how can you take care of your mind and body?_____

_____

_____

_____

_____

How well did you eat and sleep previously compared to now?

_____
_____
_____
_____
_____

What comforts you more right now? _____

_____
_____
_____
_____
_____
_____
_____
_____
_____

How would you rate your current level of grief from 0 to 10? ___

_____
_____

CHAPTER 3

Phases Of Your Betrayal Trauma Linked To Grief

*Reclaim how you grieve but grieve
like you mean it.*

The Kübler-Ross model of grief states that there are five phases to the grief process. As the betrayed partner, you may be in any stage at any moment since this is not a linear process. You will go through each of the several stages of grief on a daily basis over many days. There will be dominant phases, though, that you will eventually need to identify and consciously work through. I always say grieve like you mean it. It is your decision to intentionally take back control over your grief rather than allowing it to control you.

With a sexual-addiction-related betrayal, there would be the following phases:

- Shock and denial.
- Anger.
- Bargaining.
- Sadness and depression.
- Acceptance.

Shock and denial phase

The denial phase of grief is actually a disguised blessing.

Denial and shock are often the initial reactions you experience after the discovery or disclosure of your partner's betrayal. Denial helps you manage your emotions so you can endure the agonising suffering they cause. It is also possible you are trying to hide your true feelings behind denial or that you are trying to shut out the negative feelings—anger, pain and deep sorrow brought on by the betrayal—by maintaining a good attitude.

This is a confusing time when it is difficult for you to accept that the loss actually occurred. It is challenging to understand what happened if you are the wounded partner. At first, you might try to ignore how painful reality is, and go through the "this can't be happening, and/or it will be solved" stage. You can think that this cannot be your real life, which gives you the overwhelming urge to seek comprehension by asking your partner numerous questions over and again. Some aspects of the denial phase function as what I refer to as the "misplaced hopefulness" – when you are seeking understanding in an effort to disprove the validity of this new reality.

This stage has been characterised by some as being lifeless, of confusion, and appearing unmoved by the findings. When feelings start to surface and you are abruptly confronted with the reality of the situation, you are left only with having to completely understand what has transpired. It is normal to go about your every-day business as if everything is still the same as it was. This natural coping mechanism develops as a means of survival. The agony and shock of loss are usually too intense to grasp all at once. But moving on, acknowledging what happened, is a vital step in being better equipped and forging forward.

The depth of denial differs from individual to individual. For some of the betrayed partners, it can be quite consciously camouflaged as an attempt to process and analyse things rationally. While trying to defend or minimise their partner's actions, others are extremely direct about it – neither you nor your relationship will gain from this approach. Additionally, some betrayed partners engage in this behaviour out of a real dread of learning the exact nature of their partner's betrayal.

Creating justifications for the betrayer or accepting only what you want to believe are other examples of the denial phase. Except in cases where the denial lasts longer than is reasonable, this is a totally natural reaction. When denial persists for many years, the betrayed partner—even if they have gone through all phases of grief internally—may reach the acceptance phase. Yet, sadly, they have made the conscious decision to deny the reality and have accepted a lie.

In other words, whatever justifications you may have had for your initial denial due to the shock of your discovery, it is ok. Regarding how you experience your denial, there is no right or wrong approach. In order to proceed healthfully, what matters is how you consciously respond to your denial with radical honesty.

QUESTIONS

How did/do you experience denial? Explain. _____
_____
_____
_____
_____
_____

Did you experience misplaced hopefulness? Explain. _____
_____
_____
_____
_____
_____

Were you/are you avoiding people, places, events? Explain. _____
_____
_____
_____
_____
_____

Are you/did you minimise, justify or fully dismiss the betrayal? Explain.___

What are your feelings connected to the shock and denial of your discovery/disclosure of your partner's sexual addiction?___

Are you/were you annoyed by others' expressions of concern? Explain.___

List the aspects of the betrayal that have caused you to feel shocked, numb or avoidant. Any others? _____

_____

_____

_____

_____

_____

How would each item on the above list be answered by your mature, wiser self? _____

_____

_____

_____

_____

_____

Do you avoid questions and keep secrets about your partner's sexual addiction? Explain. _____

_____

_____

_____

_____

_____

Did you/do you hold yourself responsible for your partner's sexual addiction and the nature of your new reality? Explain._____

_____

_____

_____

_____

_____

Do you put more emphasis on your sex-addict partner than on yourself? Explain._____

_____

_____

_____

_____

To avoid judgement from others, do you act as though everything is fine? Explain._____

_____

_____

_____

_____

Can you feel the initial denial without judging yourself or those feelings?_____

_____

_____

_____

_____

_____

What words of wisdom or counsel would you offer to a younger version of yourself who was experiencing the shock and denial of their early grief? Be detailed._____

_____

_____

_____

_____

_____

_____

_____

_____

_____

CHAPTER 4

Anger Phase Of Your Betrayal Trauma Linked To Grief

A gift that can inspire transformational change is the ability to express your anger after being betrayed.

The second stage is anger, in which you become irate at your vulnerability, violation of your values and boundaries, and lack of control over what has happened. You start searching for things and people you can point the finger at. The distraught partner starts to put the past occurrences together, and gradually the truth emerges. There is clearly resentment at the foundation of the relationship being destroyed, disappointment over being let down, and rage over the betrayal. At this point, there is also the concern that your anger will alienate any remaining loved ones. As the gravity of the situation sets in, anger that has been suppressed due to fear of losing your partner or your relationship may suddenly erupt at various stages.

Given the tremendous emotional burden you are already shouldering, there may also be self-doubt and guilt, which is overwhelming. When the entire weight of betrayal sinks in, rage takes over. You may aim your anger toward your partner for the betrayal, at yourself for enabling this to occur, or both. Anger can also be misdirected and unjustly aimed toward other individuals, including kids, co-workers, and God/higher power. Moving past this stage can be challenging, and it frequently happens that a previously peaceful relationship turns aggressive.

Your body uses anger to tell you there is an injustice taking place and that something has to change for your well-being. Anger that is connected to betrayal can be communicated in one of three ways: explosion, suppression, or expression.

Breaking things, assaulting a partner, driving irrationally, using derogatory language, and throwing temper tantrums are examples of behaviours that are indicative of explosive anger. These violent outbursts bring you a lot of pain, negatively affect your relationships, employment, and may have financial, social, and/or relational repercussions.

Suppressed and internalised anger manifests as resentment. A quiet voice of anger in your mind can lead to depression, hypertension, or other health issues. It can lead to unhealthily hostile outbursts such as passive-aggressive behaviour or a consistently angry and pessimistic mindset. People who constantly put others down, criticise everything, and make cynical remarks are unable to deal with their anger in a constructive way. It is hardly surprising that they are unlikely to have many satisfying relationships.

The best method to deal with anger is to express it in a confident, non-aggressive manner. To do this, you must learn how to express your wants and needs and how to meet and honour them without attacking others. Respecting yourself and those around you requires being assertive without being overbearing or aggressive.

When you get through the anger by expressing it wholesomely, you can start to peel back the many layers of your grief. Anger is the connecting link between numbness and emotion. Do not destructively weaponise the anger your grief has caused. While being angry is totally acceptable, turning violent never is.

According to the American Psychological Association (APA, 2022), we develop our reaction to anger through social observation. This suggests that you can alter your strategy for dealing with it in the early phases of betrayal with some intentionality and effort.

How To Express Your Anger

Recognise the sources of your anger-triggers

Watch out for circumstances in your life that bother, frustrate, annoy, or anger you. Keep a list of the people, places, and things that tend to get you riled up. Knowing more about your anger-triggers will help you better manage them.

Take note of your body's reaction

People frequently assert that their anger just "appears from nowhere", despite several physical signs indicating anger is increasing. Effective anger management requires that you understand and recognise these physical warning signs or cues. The next time you feel your anger rising, focus on your body to see what you notice. Common bodily indications of anger include:
- Breathing becomes irregular or fast.
- Heart rate increases.
- Tension in the muscles.
- Clenching hands.
- Having a hot or flushed feeling or sweating.

Recognise which thoughts and beliefs are not beneficial

According to studies, a person's perspective or thought on a situation can affect how angry they feel. One or more cognitive biases may be the cause of this internal perception, which may very easily lead to an unfavourable evaluation of the circumstances and an excessively angry response. Your feelings and responses to the circumstance are significantly influenced by the self-talk you use.

Simply altering your thoughts will change your feelings, which will alter your response or behaviour. Common unhelpful thoughts include:

- **Catastrophising:** This is the act of exaggerating small problems and expecting the worst. For instance, many betrayed partners unintentionally exhibit this behaviour when a recovering addict shares their triggers while employing effective trigger-management techniques.
- **Blaming:** Assigning blame to others rather than taking responsibility for your own role in the circumstance. Even though you had nothing to do with the betrayal, you are totally responsible for your future healing and boundaries. Therefore, if you continue to disregard your boundaries and consequences despite the fact your partner is not actively seeking recovery, STOP blaming them and start looking within.
- **Overgeneralising:** Thinking in all-or-nothing, or black or white terms about the world and other people. Using the words "always", "never", and "every". For example, "I will never be safe with him/her.".

Explore and identify the feelings underneath your anger

- Question from where your anger stems. Pain? Fear? Rejection? Etc.
- Express the identified feelings and address them. What can you do to address the emerged emotion that anger triggered?
- What do you need from your partner? Express that. For example, tell your partner respectfully, "This is how I feel ...., and this is what I need......................"

Regulate your behavioural response

Some of the techniques include:
- Pause for a moment and use a time-out technique.
- Engage in deep stomach breathing.
- Engage in some form of physical activity.
- Journal.

Engage in effective communication

The best type of communication is effective listening and communication skills because it allows for the open, honest expression of feelings, opinions, and beliefs without infringing on the rights of others. To effectively communicate, it is better to state the facts as they are rather than assuming, blaming, insulting, or otherwise referring to someone badly. In this way, you can discuss how the incident affected you without disparaging anyone else. Finally, with this skill, each person attempts to understand before attempting to be understood. Always start with "I" statements without criticising, blaming or shaming your partner. For example, instead of saying, "You always make me angry when you pretend that you hear me", you could say, "I feel angry or frustrated when I am not being heard.".

When you do not express or voice your anger, it frequently internalises and turns against you. Anger is followed by guilt and depression. Instead, receive the gifts and messages that anger brings. The 14th-century poet, Hafiz, offers the reader this wisdom: "Do not surrender your grief so quickly. Let it cut more deeply. Let it season you the way few human or divine ingredients can."

In my opinion, this applies to the majority of emotions, especially anger. Let your anger cultivate the truth within you, fuel your inner strength and your heart and soul's profound integrity. The spirit of anger may be incredibly cleansing when used wisely and with humility, and it can also help you accept the reality you are facing. It might inspire you to set new boundaries, to love passionately, and to entirely surrender to what you know to be true.

QUESTIONS

List the causes of your anger over the betrayal.___

Who exactly are you angry with? Explain.___

What feelings (such as fear, pain, etc.) underlies your anger?___

What message are the underlying emotions identified above trying to convey to you?_____

_____

_____

_____

_____

_____

What can you provide yourself that these deeper emotions require?

_____

_____

_____

_____

_____

What are the most effective strategies to release your anger in healthy ways?_____

_____

_____

_____

_____

_____

What has so far assisted you the most in managing your anger?
_____
_____
_____
_____

Why is it vital to express your anger?_____
_____
_____
_____
_____

Are you angry with yourself? What are the causes?_____
_____
_____
_____
_____

Are the reasons for your self-anger (listed above) based on facts or feelings?_____
_____
_____
_____
_____
_____

Anger Phase Of Your Betrayal Trauma Linked To Grief

How did you/do you deal with your self-anger? _____

_____

_____

_____

_____

_____

Because of the betrayal, who else do you feel angry toward? Explain. _____

_____

_____

_____

_____

Express your anger toward the person who betrayed you in a letter (that you will never send them). _____

_____

_____

_____

_____

_____

In a letter, vent your anger at God or the higher authority for the betrayal that occurred?

Self-Forgiveness Is Necessary For Managing Your Betrayal Trauma Linked To Self-Anger

*To create harmony with humanity,
you must first create harmony within yourself.*

The drive to actively uphold the norms and values you want to defend comes from self-directed anger. Self-anger can be categorised with other feelings of humiliation, regret, and shame that control and shape your behaviour following betrayal. These emotions necessitate self-forgiveness, which is crucial to the development of constructive/expressive anger.

Letting go of punitive self-judgement and self-criticism over time—thoughts that feed false guilt or shame—is a necessary step toward self-forgiveness. Self-forgiveness is defined by renowned self-forgiveness researcher, Robert Enright, as "a willingness to abandon self-resentment in the face of one's own acknowledged objective wrong, while fostering compassion, generosity, and love toward oneself" (Enright, 1996, p. 115).

You can develop trust, intimacy, and emotional openness with others and with yourself by letting go of destructive self-directed anger, regret, and self-blame while improving your physical health. Numerous studies also imply that practising self-forgiveness leads to more effective conflict resolution in our romantic relationships. While self-directed anger is encouraged by unforgiveness, building self-forgiveness is a deliberate effort to combat this anger. As a result, it plays a significant role in the development of constructive and expressive anger.

How To Practise Self-Forgiveness And Therefore Eliminate Self-Anger

- **Consider the past and practise kindness and self-acceptance.** Life is not perfect and you are not a perfect being but a *human* being. Accept that you are imperfect and treat yourself with kindness and gentleness for past and current mistakes.

- **Keep in mind that suffering is a universal human experience.** Determine the specifics of what you must forgive yourself for. Make the decision to absolve yourself of responsibility for those occurrences. Have compassion for yourself and practise letting go of the notion that you are the only person in the world to go through negative experiences.

- **Take responsibility.** Assume responsibility for your past behaviour toward others and/or yourself by determining what role you played. For instance, "I take responsibility for my toxic self-blame that caused me to feel guilty for my partner's sexual addiction" or, "I acknowledge my responsibility and extend forgiveness to myself for knowing about my partner's pornography-watching but taking no action".

- **Intentional awareness and mindfulness practices to understand your emotions.** In the midst of emotional suffering, you could feel very uncomfortable. You might regularly overestimate or underestimate these emotions. The capacity to create space and quietly sit with these feelings and identify and accept them for what they are is a sign of self-compassion, which is promoted by self-forgiveness.

- **Make amends with yourself, restore your self-acceptance and empathy.** It has been found that people have trouble forgiving themselves when they lack empathy for self and others. By apologising to yourself, drawing lessons from previous difficult occurrences and growing as a person, you can restore self-acceptance, develop empathy for others as well as for yourself, and learn to embrace yourself as a fallible human.

QUESTIONS

Is it truly possible to change the past in any way? _____

_____

_____

_____

_____

_____

In hindsight, what are the things you criticise yourself for due to the insight you lacked? _____

_____

_____

_____

_____

What can you do differently if the same circumstances (as in the example above) arise in the future? _____

_____

_____

_____

_____

_____

What situations from the past have damaged your ability to forgive yourself?_____

_____

_____

_____

_____

Why were you so critical of yourself in the past? Was there a feeling of danger or pain?_____

_____

_____

_____

_____

Do you act in a way that fully demonstrates empathy for yourself and others/addicted partner? Explain._____

_____

_____

_____

_____

Describe how adopting self-forgiveness would improve your life.
_____
_____
_____
_____
_____

What in your past made you vulnerable to shame before being exposed to betrayal?_____
_____
_____
_____
_____

Write a detailed letter to yourself and include answers to these questions:

What are the things I need to forgive myself for?_____
_____
_____
_____
_____

Anger Phase Of Your Betrayal Trauma Linked To Grief

Am I ready for self-forgiveness? Explain.

_____

_____

_____

_____

_____

_____

_____

_____

_____

What kind of amendments do I need to make with myself?

_____

_____

_____

_____

_____

_____

_____

_____

_____

_____

_____

_____

What reassurances and action plan do I put in place to ensure my self-forgiveness occurs?

CHAPTER 5

Bargaining Phase Of Your Betrayal Trauma Linked To Grief

At the end, bargaining is ultimately just one piece of grief, which is the cost of love and loss that we all have to endure.

Trauma occurs when overwhelming circumstances happen to you without your consent or control. Your trauma-brain is trying to reclaim some level of control during the bargaining phase in order to lessen the impact of the overwhelming trauma reactions. Due to the sense of powerlessness and helplessness your trauma has given you, regaining control is not just crucial but a survival mechanism. The bargaining process is made worse by strong and disorderly emotions. Eventually, a barrage of messages start to infiltrate your mind, making you feel bad about yourself, angry, remorseful, ashamed and even guilty of your action or inaction, and wondering if you should have done anything different. Your mind engages in bargaining as a defence mechanism and is a form of denial. In an effort to protect you, your trauma-brain uses bargaining to fight against your painful reality.

At this stage, you frequently find yourself trapped with hypothetical scenarios and ask yourself, "if only I had stopped my partner when I saw them doing... saying... messaging... always coming home late or working late". Or, "What if I had done that instead?" Even, "What if I engage more sexually, then he/she won't look elsewhere?".

This is an effort to prevent the past betrayal or potential further hurt by picturing various scenarios or committing to new behaviours. You can be experiencing reactions of survivor guilt as a result of the traumatic betrayals. Survivor's guilt is a serious symptom of post-traumatic stress disorder (PTSD), and is frequently described as debilitating pain, guilt and shame that can leave you constantly wondering, "What might I have done differently?"

Ultimately, the grief is so excruciating that you search for ways to go back in time in an attempt to change the course of events, reclaim what you previously had, or even look for a way to find release from your suffering. The bargaining phase poses a risk of developing an addiction to remain fixed and past-oriented since it gives a brief perception of pain relief and temporary control. Your trauma-brain has a momentary fantasy about being in control and avoiding the betrayal. Though this is just fleeting, as soon as you return to the present, the pain of your reality strikes once more, making the situation feel even worse.

During The Phase Of Bargaining, You Could Feel A Variety Of Emotions:

- Pain and grief.
- Ruminating on the future or past.
- Self-loathing.
- Self-doubt.
- Guilt, self-blame and shame (due to survivor's guilt).
- Rage and resentment.
- Bitterness.
- Anger with God or higher power.
- Powerlessness to end the suffering.
- Uncertainty.
- Perfectionism.
- Controlling behaviours.
- Self-comparison to others.
- Future prognostication and pessimism.
- Judgemental attitudes (judging yourself and others).

Long-lasting grief disorder might result from a prolonged bargaining phase that is not properly addressed. This type of intense, incapacitating grief worsens rather than improves over time and prevents you from living a comfortable lifestyle. Distorted belief systems or behaviours, such as a refusal to accept reality and an attempt to oppose or reject it through rage, arguments, or bitterness, are examples of severe symptoms. Serious relationship issues for those couples who have agreed to stay together after the betrayal could result from this. All of your relationships, even the most crucial one—your relationship with yourself—will be impacted if the bargaining phase is not addressed. It will keep you in an unsafe and limbo-like state, smothering your love for you and everyone around you, keeping you in the past rather than moving forward.

Consider The Following If You Have Noticed Your Grief And The Past Trauma Are Keeping You From Moving Forward

1. Find support and maintain relationships with them to prevent loneliness or isolation.
2. Journaling as a beneficial way to release your pain and share your loss with others.
3. Set clear boundaries for yourself.
4. Find a new hobby, interest, or activity.
5. Beware of any wishful thinking about the betrayal. It is normal to imagine what life would be like if the betrayal had not occurred, but the sad fact is, that it happened.
6. Create a safe time and space to grieve properly. Accept your losses and the inevitable pain that has followed the betrayal. Allowing yourself to experience these emotions will eventually cause them to subside and lighten.
7. Consult a mental health professional for guidance.
8. Serve and stay connected to your church or other spiritual or faith-based community (if applicable).
9. Engage in self-care. Finding the right self-care strategies is crucial because grief can have an impact on both your

emotional and physical health. As a result, give priority to the behaviours and practices that will improve your general health, such as eating a balanced diet, engaging in mindfulness or meditation, regular exercise, and developing routines. Getting a good night's sleep is essential for your general well-being because sleep and mental health are strongly intertwined. Taking care of your needs can give you the courage you need to face your grief and begin the healing process.

Contrary to popular thinking, I firmly believe this phase could have advantages if you are prepared to put in the necessary effort to reap the rewards. In my professional experience, I have seen this to be true firsthand. The bargaining may serve as the start of a decision-making phase, bringing some hope for a new beginning in which one or both sides consider making new commitments. These agreements can be reached with your partner, with yourself, or with God or a higher power. This stage can encourage the establishment of healthy boundaries, whether they be personal or interpersonal. However, to navigate this significant phase and to extract valuable learnings from it, you need a great deal of awareness, professional grief processing, and support.

QUESTIONS

Complete the following statements.

I was to blame for the betrayal since I did not/I did:_____

_____

_____

_____

_____

_____

If I had done _____

_____

_____

differently, I would have had a chance to stop the betrayal.

I don't deserve a good partner or a good relationship because:

_____

_____

_____

_____

_____

Bargaining Phase Of Your Betrayal Trauma Linked To Grief

I am not good enough because:_____

_____
_____
_____
_____
_____

I had a part to play in these events in this way:_____

_____
_____
_____
_____
_____
_____

If I only would have paid more attention to:_____

_____
_____
_____
_____
_____
_____

If only I had paid closer attention to:_____

_____

_____

_____

_____

_____

_____

If only I had been more diligent when:_____

_____

_____

_____

_____

_____

_____

I need to put in more effort:

Individually: _____

_____

_____

_____

_____

Bargaining Phase Of Your Betrayal Trauma Linked To Grief

In our relationship: _____

_____

_____

_____

_____

_____

If I did more of: _____

_____

_____

_____

_____

_____

If my partner did more of: _____

_____

_____

_____

_____

_____

Or we did more of: _____

_____

_____

_____

_____

We can make it through.

My partner does not love me anymore because I am not: _____

_____
_____
_____
_____
_____

But if I change this: _____

_____
_____
_____
_____

Or this_____

_____
_____
_____

Or this_____

_____
_____
_____

about myself, my partner may not betray me again.

Bargaining Phase Of Your Betrayal Trauma Linked To Grief

If God/higher power could reverse the betrayal, I will do:_____

CHAPTER 6

Sadness And Depression Phase Of Your Betrayal Trauma Linked To Grief

It is not entirely true that time or tears will heal your pain and grief completely. But with deliberate time and thoughtful tears, you will eventually be able to carry your loss without plunging into a crippling, extended depression.

At this point in your grieving process, depression is the fourth stage that hits hard. You could begin to feel powerless and overburdened by the predicaments. You can decide to withdraw from life because you do not see the sense in going on. Yet, even though it could be very difficult, this phase of the grieving process is crucial. When someone you love betrays you with their compulsive sexual behaviours, it is only normal to experience a deep sense of loss.

When you acknowledge that the betrayal was real, depression and the knowledge of sexual addiction that can or cannot be resolved, follow. In this situation, you lament the notions of the relationship's former purity and absence of infidelity. It has been said that depression is like having a heavy, black cloud over your head, making it difficult to function, find enjoyment, or even get out of bed. Depression needs to be taken seriously, continuously monitored and, if necessary, treated by professionals.

Here, you bear the full effects of losing your sense of security in your relationship, the partner who is not who you thought they were, and a reality that no longer makes sense. The betrayal negates everything you believed. In contrast to the more cognitive and problem-solving emphasis of the previous three phases, this stage is experience- and emotion-focused. This stage could be marked by extreme melancholy and loneliness.

My most recent research on betrayed partners indicates that it is common to have intense feelings of anger, depression, and uncertainty during this time, which might give the impression that there is no way out. Some concerns include: "Has my partner ever loved me? How could I have missed any of this? How do I now move on?" As a result of these thoughts and deeper analysis of the discoveries, strong emotions are unleashed. In this trying time, everything can seem fuzzy. During this phase, you might feel that you're beginning to manage your life and that the pain of betrayal is beginning to lessen, but unanticipated realisations still occur and derail that notion. It is thought that at this time, you may reflect dejectedly on your partner's behaviour. If you are feeling sad and depressed, do not blame yourself. Being depressed is acceptable since all emotions must ultimately come to the surface in order for you to process them and heal. To discover how to move on after being betrayed, you will now need to take some time for yourself and your sadness.

Sadness And Depression Phase Of Your Betrayal Trauma Linked To Grief

Depression may even seem safe since it dulls some internal conflicts, but remaining there for an extended period of time is harmful and requires therapeutic support to overcome. Since anger is typically a secondary emotion, depression may be described as rage turned inward or all sensations silenced. Negative self-talk, denying your genuine emotions, or running away from them, leads to the build-up of unexpressed and unprocessed emotions. When you do not express your emotions in a healthy, direct manner, they wind up being retained in your body and add to system overload. As a result, your body becomes emotionally heavy as more of these feelings are suppressed, which feeds a cycle of repression that can lead to depression.

At this point, you start to understand and experience the full scope of the betrayal and the countless losses. Depression typically shows itself at this stage as insomnia, poor appetite, fatigue, lack of energy, and weeping spells. Also possible are feelings of self-pity, loneliness, isolation, emptiness, loss, and anxiety.

According to the field of emotional neuroscience, sadness is one of the seven fundamental emotions for human survival. However, maladaptive sadness and grief can have significant negative impacts on a person's life and lead to psychological issues such as major depressive disorder. Theoretically, a sustained and ongoing activation of the grieving neurological pathway can cause a cascade of neurotransmitters that suppress the reward-seeking system and cause depressive symptoms. Your trauma/grief-brain affects your memory, concentration, and cognition. This makes it challenging to carry out daily tasks since your concentration is predominantly focused on navigating the grief-related thoughts and emotions.

You may be challenged to put your attention toward overcoming your dominating sense of emptiness. This stage is marked by emptiness, perplexity, or pessimism. Actually, you have lost someone who, in a manner, was significant to you. Your former life partner—the person with whom you shared intimate moments, innermost thoughts, and secrets—might make you feel as though they have disappeared forever. Keep in mind that your spouse was not who you believed them to be, so let go of your mistaken perception of them and accept who they really were. It is ok to accept and confess that you mistakenly assumed they shared your beliefs, values, loyalty and integrity because you had the best of intentions and a good heart.

Because everything currently looks distant and unreal, you can feel as though your marriage actually never happened or that your entire intimate relationship has been a lie. Just to be clear, not all of your intimate history, memories, or past have been false. Sex addicts do not indulge in their addition 24/7, and they are very good at compartmentalisation – isolated rooms in their heads. In order to avoid the unpleasantness of contradiction, individuals may mentally separate competing thoughts, feelings, or experiences. A sex addict, for instance, has a lot of isolated rooms in their head. If they go into the room with the spouse and family, the other rooms remain locked (this could last seconds, minutes, hours, even days or months).

So, they can spend time with you, make memories, and have experiences, and then indulge in their addiction when they are away, or you are. In their minds, the two aspects exist independently. They manage to give one priority over the other even when real life and sex addiction overlap at times. Your version of your relationship with your partner is not entirely true, nor is it entirely un-true – it is both. However, once the trauma/grief-brain is activated, you enter a state in which everything is either "black or white" or in which your old life is either "real" or "unreal".

It is only reasonable to wonder how long the depressive phase will

Sadness And Depression Phase Of Your Betrayal Trauma Linked To Grief

persist. Is there any hope that the suffering and sorrow will end? Recovery from the depressive stage of the grieving process does not have a predetermined timeline. The length of time required to resume normal functioning and feelings will depend on a number of variables.

First off, how long and how intense your intimate relationship was will have a major impact on how quickly you heal. The closer, longer, or more intimate the relationship, the harder it will be to get over the grief and misery of the betrayal and the resulting losses. Additional factors to consider include the learning-circumstances and timing of them. The frequency of these episodes—as well as whether the betrayal was discovered, disclosed, or both—are some of the crucial factors. It will take longer for healing and processing since there will be more trauma and suffering as a result of additional discoveries or disclosure.

Your personality also affects how long it takes you to grieve. How you react to betrayal and losses, as well as how purposefully you work on your own recovery, will all have an impact on how long the grieving process takes. Importantly, if the sex-addict partner proactively participates as a facilitator to help their partner heal by continuing to offer transparency, therapeutic disclosure, validation of their experiences, and active work to restore the intimate relationship, the grieving partner can recover faster.

When Grieving, Depression Symptoms Can Range From Moderate To Severe And Might Include:

- Experiencing despair, hopelessness, numbness, emptiness or melancholy.
- A sense of worthlessness or guilt.
- Having trouble focusing, thinking, or making decisions.
- Being overburdened by the demands of day-to-day living.
- Excessive sleep, desire to stay in bed all day or insomnia.
- Continuous crying.
- Experiencing fatigue and low energy.
- Every remembrance of the loss being accompanied by a wave of sadness.
- Loneliness, social shame, and self-isolation – you believe people will not understand your grief.
- Losing pleasure or interest in once-favourite activities.
- Changes in appetite, weight gain or loss that is not connected to dieting.
- Suicidal or death-related ideas/thoughts.

A persistent form of severe grief can bring a prolonged depressed phase which makes it very difficult for you to cope with your losses. Thoughts could get mired in a gloomy, depressing state rather than gradually shifting to a more optimistic place. Some betrayed partners may characterise this period as emotionally crippling, rendering them with an inability to think clearly or move past the betrayal. They might feel utterly lost and abandoned.

Sadness And Depression Phase Of Your Betrayal Trauma Linked To Grief

Bewilderment, an endless feeling of sadness, excessive ruminating, negative thinking, and a continuous yearning for the past are all common emotions in this state. You could become preoccupied with your losses or the past if you have persistent depression, which makes the future seem dismal and empty.

Avoid becoming trapped in your depression by making a conscious effort to identify, honour, and process it. Major depression (severe form of depression) could set in if you remain in this phase for too long.

Let me say that again. It is important to remember that moving on does not mean forgetting the betrayal; rather, it means learning to live with the knowledge that it happened and the reality that you now need to learn to carry this knowledge. Your pain will not go away even as time passes; instead, you will discover coping with it more wholesomely.

What Should You Do To Manage The Sadness And Depression Caused By Your Grief?

- Acknowledging the need to seek assistance from a qualified therapist, friends, relatives, colleagues, spiritual leaders, and other trustworthy people cannot be overstated.

- Stay connected and continue to socialise with safe individuals. Depression typically gets worse if you withdraw from others.

- Practise processing and accepting your feelings instead of trying to suppress or escape them. Depression symptoms may be made worse by self-loathing, self-blame, or shame. An emotion can never be right or wrong. Every emotion has significant value and acts as a messenger to inform you of internal issues you need to address.

- Establish a ritual with a clear aim that will help you understand and process your grief. Establish a regular daily routine and reward yourself every day with something positive. Try to relax, practise meditation, eat a balanced diet, and engage in physical activity. You can set aside some time and space to sit by yourself and journal, compose letters to people who have wronged you (but do not mail them).

- Journaling and writing down how you feel day-to-day (moods, feelings, reactions) will help you spot patterns and understand your depression-triggers.

- Live one day at a time and wait a year before making any significant decisions.

QUESTIONS

What are some betrayal aspects that you find depressing?

_____
_____
_____
_____
_____
_____
_____
_____

What signs/symptoms of depression caused by betrayal and grief have you experienced?

Physical symptoms:_____
_____
_____
_____

Emotional symptoms: ._____
_____
_____
_____

Sexual symptoms:_____

_____

_____

_____

_____

Spiritual symptoms:_____

_____

_____

_____

Relational symptoms:_____

_____

_____

_____

Decision-making ability:_____

_____

_____

_____

_____

Sadness And Depression Phase Of Your Betrayal Trauma Linked To Grief

Self-harm or suicidal thoughts. When? For how long? _____

_____

_____

_____

_____

_____

What are some bodily signs that the sadness of betrayal has caused you? _____

_____

_____

_____

_____

_____

What are some common thoughts you experience when you are depressed? _____

_____

_____

_____

_____

_____

Before your betrayal-trauma-linked depression, how did you feel in general? _____

_____

_____

_____

_____

Do you express your emotions openly or do you suppress them?

_____

_____

_____

_____

_____

What general difficulties does depression or sadness cause you to face every day? _____

_____

_____

_____

_____

Sadness And Depression Phase Of Your Betrayal Trauma Linked To Grief

What could you have done differently to change the painful occurrences in the past?_____

_____
_____
_____
_____
_____

What are the costs of continuing to dwell on the past?_____

_____
_____
_____
_____
_____

What do you need to start letting go of from the past, and to start living in the present?_____

_____
_____
_____
_____
_____

How long has your depression lasted? _____
_____
_____
_____
_____
_____

What do you require to help you refocus on yourself and your recovery from depression? _____
_____
_____
_____
_____
_____

What kind of lifestyle changes will help with your depressive symptoms? _____
_____
_____
_____
_____
_____

Sadness And Depression Phase Of Your Betrayal Trauma Linked To Grief

Do you allow yourself enough leisure time and self-care? _____

_____
_____
_____
_____
_____

How are you investing in your mental health? _____

_____
_____
_____
_____
_____

What are three healthy coping mechanisms you use? _____

_____
_____
_____
_____
_____

CHAPTER 7

Acceptance Phase Of Your Betrayal Trauma Linked To Grief

While accepting losses does not imply denying them, it might help you progressively adjust to your new reality by offering you a positive outlook on life.

Acceptance

The fifth and final stage of your grief is related to acceptance. During this last phase, you begin to accept your personal and relational losses and the circumstances preceding them. This does not imply that you endorse or support any of it. You are finally able to accept the reality of what has happened and begin to look for avenues to move on. It is important that during this stage you accept how this loss has changed your life and stop wishing for everything to go back to how it used to be. Your life is forever changed, and it is now time to seek out new meaning.

Acceptance does not imply justification for or satisfaction from one's losses. Although I do not personally know many people who are at ease with betrayal and the ensuing infidelities, this stage is about realising that this new reality cannot be reversed or fought against.

This phase is confronting you with a new reality which, depending on the information you have gathered, is your current reality forever, whether you like it or not. The only thing left for you to do is learn how to cope with this new, unwanted and bitter but ongoing reality. During this phase, you will find yourself saying, "it is what it is" more frequently and "I don't want this f***ing reality" less frequently.

This phase seems to be the most unique and distinctively individualised of all the stages. In comparison to the betrayed partner, who would experience grieving for a much longer period of time, the addict partner may reach this phase much sooner, especially if they are making progress in their recovery. A couple who encounters this discrepancy may go through very trying and difficult times as they move through the darkness at very different paces. It will be detrimental to the betrayed partner's mental health and intimate relationship if the recovering addict conveys impatience and pushes them to move past the betrayal quickly. Acceptance entails developing new perspectives on what happened and how it may affect the future. Instead of a flawless conclusion, lasting closure, or approval of the betrayal, it is a phase of transition following a major shift.

It is possible that you will begin to have thoughts like, "I know

Acceptance Phase Of Your Betrayal Trauma Linked To Grief

what happened and can understand the causes", "This had nothing to do with me and was entirely the result of my partner's addiction and choices", "I am able to forgive and move on" or "I can't forgive and move on but I will move out" etc. Right now, the past does not matter as much as the present and the future. New-found hope is a result of the new attitude and relationships.

How you move on in this phase is once again related directly to the nature of the loss, how resilient you are to grief, and the support networks you have in place. The order and experience with these phases will differ from one individual to the next, but that does not mean they are any less important. If you become stuck in one stage or are unable to cope with the loss over a long period of time, you might need to seek the assistance of a trained professional.

Processing then proceeding to acceptance

You'll notice that many of your emotions are inflamed and triggered when your spouse's sexual addiction and deceptions are uncovered.

True acceptance calls for the betrayed partner to be given a safe place in which to process and express their emotions, and for the betrayer to acknowledge and validate those emotions. The offender must also guarantee that such harm will not happen again. The betrayed partner must take these steps on their own, but the offender must undertake them first and foremost if they are still in a relationship. If this process is omitted, and the early, negative emotions associated with the betrayal are repressed, this will continue to negatively impact the betrayed partner and relationship. As a result, harmful side effects such as grief, rage, contempt, humiliation, and shame will be generated. You will be able to assess how you are managing the betrayal-trauma and related grief once you have gained true perspective.

True perspective can only come about when the betrayal-related emotions are identified, appreciated, acknowledged, validated, and surrendered. This point of view could assist you in deciding whether or not the relationship can recover from the betrayal and continue to grow.

Acceptance does not include denying or forgetting the betrayal ever happened. Additionally, it does not mean that you will no longer be hurting over your losses. Acceptance means acknowledging the present as it is, with all of the good and not so good that it provides, in order to have an impact on your future. It is more like letting yourself experience reality as if it was an unwanted gift that you could not manage to part with.

In my study, I found a bitter truth that time does not heal all wounds caused by intimate betrayal. Even after the initial bleeding stops, the anguish persists. While time will not completely heal all of the wounds caused by betrayal, it might help you gradually learn to hold space for your grief and carry it without becoming paralysed.

Acceptance requires taking ownership

Without a doubt, the betrayal has altered you and your life forever. Your responsibilities may start to shift during the acceptance phase as you can develop new interests, relationships, and objectives. You can also choose to eliminate or allocate responsibilities and tasks to others. Acceptance typically comes as you gradually take responsibility for your goal-setting, self-care, boundaries, and recovery. Acceptance can initially mean having fewer bad days than good. Moreover, you are more receptive to altering some behaviours in this context in order to honour and meet your own needs. In this space, you connect to and feel comfortable with your emotions with an increased capacity and competency to address them. Most importantly, instead of adhering to what is deemed "normal" by others, you gradually establish the normal that is optimal for you. Acceptance may take the form of telling yourself things like, "I'll acknowledge my anger and what its message is actually about" or "I'll forgive myself if I don't manage to finish all my pre-planned tasks". Alternatively, "It's ok for me to feel sad; how could I not feel sad after suffering betrayal?"

The fundamental goal of the acceptance phase is to embrace that your new reality exists, that you have no authority over it, and that it has an impact on your relationships and the course of your life.

The Following Are Some Hallmarks Of The Grief Process' Acceptance Phase

- Accepting reality for what it is—right now—not what you anticipated it to be.
- Increasing your sense of presence and awareness (mindfulness).
- Becoming more positive and optimistic.
- Practising self-care and self-compassion.
- Searching for deeper purpose.
- Having the capacity to endure, sitting in emotions, and showing vulnerability.
- Feeling more comfortable and confident.
- Responding as opposed to reacting to the circumstances.
- Using transparent, direct, and real interactions.
- Establishing healthy coping mechanisms.

The best and worst parts of the past can both be carried forward in the spirit of acceptance.

Acceptance is a manner of living consciously rather than arriving at a specific destination – one that is both insightful and meaningful. This is not meant to encourage you to approve or be delighted or grateful with your suffering. It is acknowledging that the betrayal and the associated suffering are a part of your past, as well as elements of your current wisdom.

True acceptance makes it possible for you to build a safe haven that is totally accepting of your past, along with all the pain and suffering that comes with it. To all the experiences, narratives, and relationships connected to your losses that have lingered into the present, and the ways in which suffering and loss have influenced who you are now. Yes, the way your story has played out has been beyond your control, but you get to choose how you move forward from this point.

Real acceptance is a progressive process and happens when functioning resumes with fewer, more manageable triggers that are no longer debilitating.

Many, but not all, betrayed partners reach acceptance by being able to gradually forgive the offender and themselves. Forgiveness is like freeing oneself from all the negative feelings associated with the betrayal/infidelity and being able to move forward either within the relationship or external to the relationship. In this space you have **collected** all the real parts of your relationship, you have **connected** all the puzzle pieces and now you choose to **correct** your mindset and perspective to reclaim your own destiny.

Acceptance and forgiveness process

Forgiveness is not always togetherness.

When you reach the acceptance phase, forgiveness emerges. This includes forgiving both the one who deceived you, and yourself. The importance of self-forgiveness has received a lot of attention lately. People tend to frequently assert that they have forgiven themselves for a range of offences. For instance, wrongs done to them as well as to others, failing to recognise deceit or betrayal done to them, self-directed wrongs resulting from some sort of personal weakness or failure, or failing to respect relational boundaries that could have provided relational certainty.

Self-forgiveness fulfils two crucial self-interested goals for the betrayed partner. First of all, even in the absence of the offender's remorse, it succeeds in its objective of returning the fundamental moral agency to the betrayed. Second, self-forgiveness is an extension of forgiveness for others and a way to maintain or reclaim one's essential self-worth, self-compassion and self-love. Self-forgiveness is a non-linear process that aids in improving your comprehension of the wrongdoing/betrayal and how it has affected you on a fundamental level. Next, you decide to consciously work through the process of forgiving yourself, deal with your negative self-talk, and cultivate self-compassion. Once more, in this context, you will gradually obtain a wider perspective on your experiences.

How do you forgive the one who betrayed you?

Forgiving is not forgetting, excusing, justifying, denying, tolerating or endorsing the wrongdoing.

When you pardon the one who deceived you, what exactly does forgiveness offer you? It is difficult to understand this and often seems like an impossible undertaking to extend a second chance to someone who has wronged you and broken your heart. It can be more appealing to hold your justified resentment inside and let it fester, using your pain to demonstrate to your partner the great harm they did to you. Your suffering can lead you to believe that the only way to find relief is to ensure the person who caused your pain also suffers, as that would be the only possible form of justice. But the person who would suffer the most would be you. You are imprisoned in this area by an invisible barrier with sharp edges that keeps you in pain and, worse, prevents you from moving forward. Unhealed pain frequently manifests as unrestrained pain directed at self and others. Your pain will constrict and eventually eventually take control the more you concentrate on it.

How do you start your unique forgiveness process?

You may choose forgiveness in order to be free of victimisation, bitterness, resentment, and sadness once more. However, it is one of those things where talking about it is easier than actually doing it. Forgiving someone is challenging when you are still resentful. It consequently becomes more difficult to forgive oneself due to the internal hatred you are harbouring. There are two parts to forgiving: a choice and an action. You might be asking how you can deal with your pain and still be forgiving. You choose to sit with the pain the offender has caused you, accept that suffering, and validate it. Then, reframe your narrative to acquire fresh insights into your reality. Choose a new way of thinking in order to experience the healing that comes with forgiveness rather than attempting to move at a particular pace or arrive at a specific destination.

On occasion, you might need to extend a small amount of forgiveness in order to move along the process. Or, it could be necessary to offer a little bit of forgiveness several times a day, and with the possibility and self-permission to retract it at any time. Exactly how you please. This is a unique and non-linear process, and how it plays out will vary from person to person. You follow your own path of forgiving without listening to advice from others about when and how to do so. For example, if you choose to remain after being betrayed and try to restore the relationship, that is forgiveness even if you never express it verbally. When you reflect on the past and are no longer filled with stomach-turning agony or a desire for vengeance, you are progressing in the forgiveness process.

Forgiveness comes from processing your suffering and pain until there is nothing left (or whatever is left is easily manageable) but compassion – compassion for yourself, compassion for life, and compassion for your betrayer. Nevertheless, forgiving someone is extremely challenging if you do not have mercy and compassion. Furthermore, it can be difficult to feel empathy for your partner after they treated you so savagely. As a result, rather than making an effort to be forgiving at once, start by allowing yourself to feel compassionate and humane for the pain that motivated their choices and actions. Again, it is ok if this approach does not work for you. Make the decision to keep an open mind, stay in touch with your authentic self, and evaluate what works for you and what does not.

Some betrayed partners believe that forgiveness includes a second chance for their relationship, their children, or even for themselves as individuals, rather than just for the offender. Allow yourself the gift of reconciliation if you choose that road while maintaining appropriate boundaries to ensure your ongoing relational safety and honour. You could create a more conscious and intimate relationship. It is normal to be fearful and have all the what ifs circulating in your head. However, this time you choose you, and give yourself a second chance if you wish, and without any external judgement or force.

On the other hand, even if a relationship has ended, you can still forgive from a distance.

I often say: "Forgiveness is not always togetherness."

You may choose to *unconditionally* forgive your addicted partner whenever you are ready – without regard to how they react and without any time pressures. This implies that you are willing to forgive even in the absence of an apology or change of behaviour (which, of course, requires a serious safety or exit plan).

For other betrayed partners, they *condition* their forgiveness based on the betrayer's sincere repentance. There is no right or wrong way to forgive; honour your unique journey, regardless of the type of forgiveness you are willing to offer. When you choose to forgive, keep in mind that forgiveness is not always followed by re-establishing trust. Because trust is a completely *conditioned* process and depends on consistent, concrete indications of change that fosters relational safety. To put it another way, trust requires consistency in the alignment of words and actions. If you attach trust and forgiveness with one another, you face a greater chance of going through more suffering in the future.

Without a doubt, forgiveness promotes better health, better relationships, and an all-around more optimistic attitude on life. Who would not desire better overall health and life quality?

Given that one aspect of forgiveness, like love, is the emotional component of it rather than being just a concept, a philosophy, or just a combination of processes, forgiveness presents an issue that is not typically acknowledged. Like falling in love, genuine forgiving involves a great deal of emotional patience and readiness, and some elements of sporadic attitude.

Do not pressure yourself to forgive before you are ready. Rushing through the process of forgiving is similar to trying to prevent water from passing through your hands.

If you still find it easier to be angry, vindictive, or unwilling than forgiving, then you are not ready, and that is totally fine. You must have mentally and emotionally prepared yourself for forgiveness—if it ever comes to you—by allowing yourself to fully grieve the wrongs.

While Forgiveness Cannot Be Rushed, There Are Several Ways To Encourage It

- **Stop forcing yourself to forgive.** You are not required to forgive your partner's or anyone else's bad decisions. This in no way implies that you lack moral character. Because betrayal causes countless injuries, it takes longer than any other grief to heal.
- **Acknowledge and validate all feelings and learn to express freely but safely.** This does not imply having emotional reactions. It includes feeling every sensation you are experiencing while also being conscious of and accepting them.
- **Intentionally identify and process each phase of your grief.** The more you try to escape your painful

sentiments, the more they will cling to you. Embrace the dichotomy; try to sit with your pain and validate it so that it passes more swiftly and effectively.

- **Notice your feelings and name them.** Do you feel resentful, furious, violated, betrayed, wounded? It is more calming to express your emotions in the here and now rather than thinking about the past.

- **Put an end to seeking revenge.** Disallow any thoughts of harming the wrongdoer in retaliation or retribution, as well as vengeance. Back and forth retaliation simply makes your own suffering greater.

- **Take into account your partner's addiction.** Try to understand the underlying issues and early trauma that led to their poor attitude and choices. (This does not in any way justify their deception and betrayal.)

- **Ask yourself if you are prepared to choose to forgive, even just a little.** Forgiveness is an emotion, a decision, and a proactive, empowering action. It is also not a one-time choice or action. You might have to make repeated intentional decisions to conduct it.

Acceptance Phase Of Your Betrayal Trauma Linked To Grief

QUESTIONS

Write a goodbye letter to the relationship you thought you had.

_____
_____
_____
_____
_____
_____
_____
_____
_____
_____
_____
_____
_____
_____

Saying goodbye makes you feel: _____

_____
_____
_____
_____

The betrayal has taught you these positive lessons about yourself:
_____
_____
_____
_____
_____
_____

About you: _____
_____
_____
_____

About the old relationship we had: _____
_____
_____
_____

I want you to know that I am determined to: ___
_____
_____
_____
_____

Acceptance Phase Of Your Betrayal Trauma Linked To Grief

I know there is nothing I could have done to prevent or reverse what has happened. Therefore, my plan is to cope well with this new reality by: _____

_____

_____

_____

_____

_____

How can you employ a healthy perspective of your experiences of the betrayal? _____

_____

_____

_____

_____

_____

Are you employing intentionality to replace any unhelpful thoughts and perspective associated with the betrayal? Explain how. _____

_____

_____

_____

_____

What does 'acceptance' of betrayal look like in day-to-day life for you? _____

_____

_____

_____

How do you avoid getting stuck in the past or feeling anxious about the future? _____

_____

_____

_____

Are you still holding to some negative emotions that are making you stuck in life? What are those? _____

_____

_____

_____

What do you need to address them? _____

_____

_____

_____

_____

Acceptance Phase Of Your Betrayal Trauma Linked To Grief

What are the pros and cons of holding on to them? _____
_____
_____

What would you advise your best friend to do in the same situation?
_____
_____

List the reasons you deem necessary for you to accept (not approve or like) the betrayal? _____
_____
_____
_____

Professionally: _____
_____

Relationally: _____
_____

Spiritually: _____
_____

Sexually: _____
_____

Your outlook on life: _____
_____

How would acceptance help you achieve any goals in life?_____

_____

_____

_____

_____

_____

What are you blaming yourself for and what do you hear your judgemental-self saying?_____

_____

_____

_____

_____

The way you feel about yourself with regard to this situation, or in general, is?_____

_____

_____

_____

_____

_____

_____

What does this statement mean to you?

I lovingly recognise and accept my feelings and judge them no more.

_____

_____

_____

_____

_____

_____

_____

_____

I own my feelings. No one can make me feel anything. My feelings are:

_____

_____

_____

_____

_____

_____

_____

_____

What does this statement mean to you?

Regarding the betrayal, I am feeling part GUILT (remorse over what I have done) and part SHAME (remorse over who I am or have become). _____

_____

_____

_____

_____

_____

_____

_____

My guilt over the betrayal is appropriate/inappropriate because?

_____

_____

_____

_____

_____

_____

_____

Acceptance Phase Of Your Betrayal Trauma Linked To Grief

What does this statement mean to you?

As I really examine how I feel about myself, I realise that underlying my feeling of shame, there is a belief or a set of beliefs that I hold about myself that are not true. _____

_____
_____
_____
_____
_____
_____
_____

What do I need to forgive myself for? _____

_____
_____
_____
_____
_____

I deserve self-forgiveness because: _____

_____
_____
_____
_____
_____

Are you ready to start the process of releasing the need to blame yourself and to be right, and are you WILLING to see the perfection in what is just the way it is? _____

_____

_____

_____

_____

What feelings do you need to release from your consciousness to start the process of self-forgiveness? _____

_____

_____

_____

_____

How did your partner's upbringing affect their lives and behaviours at the time of betrayal? _____

_____

_____

_____

_____

Acceptance Phase Of Your Betrayal Trauma Linked To Grief

List any positive emotions you may have for your partner who betrayed you. _____

_____

_____

_____

Are you ready to start the process of forgiving the one who betrayed you? _____

_____

_____

How would forgiving the offenders (including your partner) mean and look like for you? _____

_____

_____

_____

_____

How can you forgive the unforgiveable? _____

_____

_____

_____

What are the obstacles that prevent you from starting the forgiveness process? _____

_____

_____

_____

Do you think the restoration and recovery work of you and your partner is indicative of initiation of the forgiveness process? Explain.

_____

_____

_____

_____

What do you need from the offender in order to consider granting them forgiveness? _____

_____

_____

_____

Acceptance Phase Of Your Betrayal Trauma Linked To Grief

Is your offending partner worthy of your forgiveness? Explain.

_____

_____

_____

_____

_____

I am ready to grant forgiveness/not grant my forgiveness because:

_____

_____

_____

_____

Describe how the injustice of the betrayal you experienced and your efforts to forgive, have helped you grow: _____

_____

_____

_____

How has the betrayal affected your worldview? _____

_____

_____

_____

How has forgiving (or not forgiving) the one who betrayed you affected the way in which you perceive the world? _____

_____

_____

_____

_____

_____

Are you more resilient than you were prior to choosing whether or not to forgive? _____

_____

_____

_____

_____

_____

What future changes in relational trust would there be should you forgive or not? _____

_____

_____

_____

_____

_____

Acceptance Phase Of Your Betrayal Trauma Linked To Grief

Do you believe that your and your partner's efforts at healing and restoration constitute a start to the forgiveness process? _____

_____

_____

_____

_____

_____

What happens if you choose not to forgive? _____

_____

_____

_____

How can you tell whether you have started the forgiveness process? Give your response to this statement: _____

_____

_____

_____

_____

_____

_____

_____

By escaping or ignoring the anguish that comes with betrayal and the complex losses it causes, you surrender your power and control.

Take the time you need to understand what your anger is really about. Allow anger to energise you in your quest for what is right and true for you. Ultimately, it is not really about the other person who made you angry, it is about utilising the situation to discover a deeper level of insight and truth within yourself.

CHAPTER 8

Healing From Betrayal Trauma In A Nutshell

After being betrayed, the world can appear cold and merciless. Do not let this prevent you from experiencing life's delights beyond betrayal.

Despite the fact that dealing with betrayal-related grief and all of the losses it entails is a necessary part of life, there are ways to alleviate the pain, process your emotions in a cognisant and active way, accept your grief, and finally discover a new perspective on life and move forward.

- **Regardless of your gender, actively seek out professional help for processing your betrayal-trauma and associated grief.** According to data, 90% of those who sought therapy for issues related to their mental health indicated that their symptoms and quality of life had improved. It is imperative for your long-term wellness, and non-negotiable if you are a male-betrayed partner to get expert support and persevere through the process. Research has shown that men are less likely than women to seek professional help. Men are twice as slow to pursue support for mental issues than women, and twice as many women as men attend therapy. Traditional masculine "norms", cultural expectations, and stigma all have a negative impact on the way men seek help.

Some of the internalised or traditional ideas of what it means to be "manly", include: powerful, prosperous, a provider, independent, in control, and competent. Such viewpoints place a strong focus on the necessity to restrain one's emotions and make an effort to avoid needing assistance. For a male, receiving counselling could be seen as feeling helpless, powerless, weak, vulnerable, marginalised, and "unmanly". The ability to communicate one's feelings freely has historically been more prevalent in women. Men commonly hold the opinion that details of their private lives, such as their health, romantic relationships, and family business, should not be disclosed.

For many years, guys have been given the incorrect message that "men don't cry" and that if they do, no one should notice it. As a result, many men minimise their symptoms and suffering while they are coping with problems with their physical or mental health.

For some men, it is easier to avoid and minimise the issue than it is to admit it exists and take the necessary steps to address it. Even though all of the factors mentioned play a significant role in men's reluctance to seek help, research shows that the majority of men who do seek therapy view the healing process as a valiant struggle from which they emerged considerably stronger.

- **Give yourself permission to postpone making important decisions.** Do not base important decisions on fleeting feelings brought on by shock and grief caused by betrayal *(if you are in an abusive relationship, run, get out now)*. Make that determination to postpone making decisions about your relationship or life until you have made some more healing progress. Uncontrolled actions and decisions made in the midst of your shock and suffering can undermine any future chances for co-parenting, a peaceful breakup, or an underlying desire to mend the relationship. You may have decided to take revenge in another way, such as telling friends and family about your partner's infidelity or by having your own revenge-affair.

  Like you, many betrayed partners have come to realise that their decisions were driven more by anger and pain than by their underlying principles and convictions. When your emotions are strongly felt, you are more inclined to take extreme actions that you could come to regret. Many betrayed partners struggle with the decision of whether to end their relationship or try to rebuild a good one. Your quick decisions could simply be knee-jerk reactions brought on by the intensity of your suffering. **Pause.**

- **Do not hold back any of your emotions; accept them all; cry if you want to.** Keep in mind that you have experienced a tremendous tragedy. In your initial shock at what has happened, you might reject the truth. Since nothing is organised in a single place anymore, life feels dispersed. Validate your pain and honour your journey without comparing how you are processing your grief. Take into account that your grief process is personal and unique to you. You may want to cry a lot, which could be a huge relief and release during grief.

- **Healing from trauma and grief processing takes time.** Even after you start to accept your losses, it is common to still experience periodic depression, anger, sadness or feelings of being overwhelmed. A variety of unanticipated and complex emotions that need processing might be triggered by grief. Look for face-to-face professional support. Try to process through the phases of grief consciously and be aware that sometimes it will not be simple to accept what has happened. This is ok because with practise and mindfulness, acceptance becomes simpler.

- **Find equilibrium.** Take on only what you can handle. You should be aware of when a pause is necessary. At any time, allow yourself to say NO. Take the time and space to engage in something enjoyable and relaxing.

- **Bring the focus back on you, take care of your body and mind, cultivate an attitude of gratitude and mindfulness.** It is easy to get completely focused with your addict partner as your anxieties through post-discoveries, grow. Distress about making the right choices can result in preoccupations with attending to your partner's addiction, recovery needs, or demands. They also include worries that your partner is still capable of lying and causing further harm. These perceived threats that follow betrayal can become all-consuming. The risk in these situations is that you may fully sacrifice your personal needs in an effort to save your spouse or the relationship. This approach is not the cure it may first appear to be, and actually hurts your relationship and health.

  Do not try to drive your addict partner's recovery bus, and please do not become an enabler either. Establish and keep boundaries in your current relationships, develop a self-care plan, and don't forget to focus on your healing and needs. Furthermore, your emotionality will show up in your physicality. Consequently, when you take care of your physical health, you are also taking care of your emotional health. It is crucial to place your attention on the positives, on what is going right in your life, comforting memories, new insights, what you have rather than what you have lost, and the fortitude and resiliency you have demonstrated.

The sadness brought on by betrayal and grief can be helped to heal with the aid of various mindfulness techniques. By engaging in mindfulness practices, you can develop the ability to accept and cherish each moment without avoiding or suppressing any of the feelings that arise, including happiness, gratitude, sadness, pain, and heartbreak.

The grieving process can be helped by employing mindfulness practices including journaling, mindful breathing, and meditation. A technique that is effective for lowering body tension or soothing an anxious mind is mindful deep breathing. You can practise anywhere at any time, all you need to do is concentrate on your body as your breath comes in and goes out.

Yoga, meditation, and other relaxation techniques all revolve around paying attention to the breath. As long as it is done correctly, with attention and concentration on your breathing and body, you can apply this technique whenever you wish to calm your body and mind. Learning the principles of mindful breathing can improve your control over your heart rate, blood pressure, and anxiety while also helping you manage chronic pain.

> **How To Practise Mindful Breathing:**
> - Sit up straight in a chair or on the floor and find a comfortable position to relax.
> - Eyes closed or looking down.
> - Feel free to have some relaxing, gentle music in the background.
> - Place your right hand over your heart and your left hand over your stomach. As you breathe in and out, pay attention to how your stomach and chest move. Pay attention to the air in your nostrils as well as the warmth of your breath as it leaves your body.
> - For a few minutes, keep paying close attention to your breath in this manner.
> - Your mind will wander from time to time, so when it does, simply acknowledge it, accept it without passing judgement, and gently bring your attention back to your breathing and body.

Practising mindful meditation is non-negotiable. Mindful meditation has been practised from the beginning of time. This helpful tool can assist you in managing the difficulties in life caused by betrayal and grief. Relearning how to slow down and turn inward while taking a "mental break" has become more and more common. That could be, at least in part, attributed to the known cognitive benefits of meditation. The process of practising mindfulness, simply put, is being cognisant of where your conscious attention is focused. The thoughts that surface could be positive or negative. But as you work on this inward journey with non-judgemental focus, you will be able to access a peace that already resides inside of you.

To achieve a higher state of serenity, anyone can begin mindful meditation practise. This is a practise of pausing, paying attention and turning inside. Mindful meditation is an expression of love and compassion for oneself. It allows you to practise being present, non-judgemental, and curious while paying attention to how you are feeling in the moment. It might be difficult and overwhelming to sit with your thoughts and feelings during meditation, but by doing so, you can make a space for yourself where you can reconnect with your body and mind, facilitate re-integration, and discover healing.

There are various meditation techniques, and the practise can be done in any method. The fundamentals for any type of meditation are to choose a calm, peaceful environment, adopt a comfortable posture, avoid distractions, and concentrate on your breathing. You alone make the practise unique, and it can be modified to fit your needs and individuality.

Benefits Of Meditation After Two Months

- The findings strongly imply that just two months of meditation is sufficient to change the way your brain functions, potentially promoting increased focus, emotional control, and intentional decision-making.

- In 2011, a Harvard research team found that mindfulness meditation can actually change the structural makeup of the brain. After eight weeks of mindfulness meditation, the hippocampus, which regulates learning and memory, as well as various areas of the brain involved in emotion regulation and self-awareness processing, showed increased cortical thickness and functioning.

- Cultivates neuroplasticity. An increasingly well-known term that refers to the brain's capacity to continuously restructure and alter throughout your lifespan, explains

how mindful meditation can result in physical changes in the brain.
- Decreases triggers, and fight/flight/freeze responses.
- Improves concentration and attention.
- Reduces activity in the default mode network, or "monkey mind" – the part of the brain that controls ruminating and anxious thinking. Betrayed partners want to reduce mind-wandering because it is frequently linked to being unhappy, pondering, and stressing about the past and the future.
- Lessens pain, anxiety, and depressive symptoms.
- Increases one's sense of overall well-being.
- Greater release of beneficial brain chemicals such as serotonin, melatonin and endorphin, which all contribute to the ability to relax and focus.
- An increasing body of research has demonstrated that meditation can be highly successful in assisting people in overcoming various types of addictions and compulsive behaviours due to its impact on the brain's self-control areas.

The more you meditate, the more quickly your brain will be rewired to achieve a serene Zen state. Your abilities will improve as you put them to use more frequently. Even if you can only meditate for a short period of time, you may release stress, sharpen your focus, and become more conscious of your body and mind.

How To Practise Mindful Meditation

1. Locate a peaceful area and take a seat on a cushion or chair. Put your legs in whatever position feels most comfortable to you. Try stretching or crisscrossing them out in front of you. Feel free to set up a meditation cushion. This cushion, often referred to as a zafus (one with curved edges), helps keep you grounded and comfortable as you meditate.

2. Place your hands down in a relaxed position, let them rest naturally and try not to think about what they are doing. Some people choose to have their hands in the mudra position (with the thumb and pointer finger squeezed together), while others like to maintain their hands folded in their laps. Do whatever makes you most comfortable.

3. Close your eyes, tuck your chin in and focus inwards. A small chin tilt aids with chest opening, and closing your eyes eliminates visual disturbances. Because it facilitates meditation and helps you focus internally, this position is ideal. With enough practise, you can become adept at meditating while keeping your eyes open.

4. Pay close attention to your deep breathing. This is the primary objective of meditation. Instead of attempting to avoid thinking, give yourself something uplifting to consider, like your breath. Let your problems float away as you focus on your inhalation and exhalation. Close your mouth and breathe through your nose. Try not to clench your jaw or grind your teeth. Focus on the sensation of air moving through your nostrils or the expansion and contraction of your lungs.

5. Slowly scan your body for any sensations. Take note of your body's many breathing points, such as your chest, belly, and nose. Be aware of your thoughts but let them go rather than lingering on or analysing them. This is possible if you bring your attention to the here and now and to your breathing. The goal is to just be present in each breath. Focus on just one breath at a time when your mind wanders. Stay in this state for 10 or more minutes.

- **Reconnect and do not disconnect from others.** The belief that sexual-addiction-related betrayal only happens in severely broken relationships, as a result of your own failures, or in morally corrupt people, makes it easy to isolate. However, in actuality, sexual addiction does not discriminate, predates intimate relationships, and even manifests itself in relationships that are perceived to be successful. Because your spouse cheated on you, you might feel humiliated or ashamed. You could find it challenging to talk to a friend, family member, or even a mental health professional as a result of these feelings. Finding the proper support can also be challenging because in some cases, well-meaning people may advise you to end your relationship despite the fact your partner may be committed to doing recovery and relationship restoration, or they may put pressure on you to stay when your partner shows no signs of safety or recovery. Therefore, during this trying time, keep a few safe people close rather than isolating yourself (which increases shame). Safe people are those who will not push you and will simply provide support while giving you the freedom, time and space to decide for yourself. Let them know how they can support you, then accept their support.

- **Post-betrayal growth for both you, your partner, and your relationship is possible.** Start thinking about and making plans for the future when you are ready. Should you experience some sadness, remorse or disappointment if things do not go as planned, you will soon accept the reality instead of denying or fighting it. Discover new meaning, sense of direction, and purpose. After learning about your partner's sexual addiction, you may decide to reconcile; however, the notion that "he/she is my special person and will never betray me" is no longer real, which means that many aspects of your relationship will never feel the same again. Yet, if both you and your spouse are prepared for it, the painful experience of betrayal may be turned into a positive lesson to help you learn more about who you are, what you want, and how the world works. Following betrayal brought on by sexual addiction, numerous relationships have grown stronger and more intimate. No doubt betrayal has changed your life but that does not mean its meaning has vanished. Discover who you are and take note of the activities you once loved but no longer do, the ones you still find enjoyable, and the ones you have always wanted to try but have not.

QUESTIONS

Write a thank you and goodbye letter to your grief. Use separate paper so you can read it a couple of times and process it with your therapist. Then burn it. _____
_____
_____
_____
_____
_____

Write down three specific examples of when you have felt betrayed the most. _____
_____
_____
_____
_____
_____
_____

How does it make you feel? _____

_____

_____

_____

_____

_____

_____

_____

_____

_____

In which part of your body do you feel it? _____

_____

_____

_____

_____

_____

_____

What number is it at? (1 minimum–7 maximum) _____

_____

_____

Of the three examples, identify the first you wish to work on. (Apply the following 1 to 3 tapping steps.) _____

_____
_____
_____
_____
_____
_____
_____

Identify the next example that you want to explore and apply the following 1 to 3 tapping steps. _____

_____
_____
_____
_____
_____
_____
_____
_____

1. Now, start tapping on the side of the hand (Karate chop point) while speaking aloud your statement:

   "Even though I feel betrayed about *(insert the betrayal)* _____

   _____

   and I can feel it in my *(body part)* _____

   and it is at a number *(add number)*_____

   and it makes me feel *(feelings and sensations)*_____

   _____

   _____,

   I deeply and completely love and accept myself. I choose to release the pain."

2. Then tap on the facial and upper body points using the phrases that include information on the story name, number and feeling while speaking aloud the reminder phrases:

   • Eyebrow: I feel betrayed about *(what you are betrayed about)*

   _____

   • Side of eye/temple: I can feel it in my *(body part)*_____

   _____

   • Under the eye: It is at a number *(number)*_____

   _____

   • Under the nose: It makes me feel *(feeling or sensation)*____

   _____

- Chin: In my *(body part)* _____
  at a number *(number)*_____
- Collarbone: Really *(feeling or sensation)*_____
  _____

3. Then relax. Take a gentle breath in and out and then a sip of water. Ask yourself, "What number is the pain of betrayal at?" If reduced to a level you feel happy with, you can stop. Otherwise, ask yourself what is left about the betrayal.

Felt betrayed because:_____
_____
_____
_____
_____
_____
_____

Where in the body do you feel it?_____
_____
_____
_____

On a scale of 1 to 7, what number is it at?_____
_____

How does it make you feel?_____

_____

_____

_____

_____

_____

_____

_____

_____

Repeat steps 1-3 till the charge on what made/makes you feel betrayed comes down. Once this example is complete, go back and explore the remaining two examples.

What are three of your most cherished personal values?_____

_____

_____

_____

_____

_____

_____

_____

What is the meaning of life?_____

_____

_____

_____

_____

_____

_____

_____

_____

_____

What is your personality type?_____

_____

_____

_____

_____

_____

_____

_____

_____

_____

Did you make time for yourself this week? _____

_____
_____
_____
_____
_____
_____

Are you making time for your social life? _____

_____
_____
_____
_____
_____
_____

What scares you the most right now? _____

_____
_____
_____
_____
_____
_____

What is something you find inspiring?_____
_____
_____
_____
_____
_____
_____

What is something that brings you joy?_____
_____
_____
_____
_____
_____
_____

When was the last time you gave back to others?_____
_____
_____
_____
_____
_____
_____

What matters most to you right now? _____

_____
_____
_____
_____
_____
_____

What is something you would like to do more of and why? _____

_____
_____
_____
_____
_____
_____

What is something you would like to do less of and why? _____

_____
_____
_____
_____
_____
_____

What three words describe you best? _____

_____
_____
_____
_____
_____

What keeps you awake at night? _____

_____
_____
_____
_____
_____

What do you need to do to address those issues that keep you awake at night? _____

_____
_____
_____
_____
_____
_____

How important is your physical health to you? _____

_____
_____
_____
_____
_____

How important is your mental health to you? _____

_____
_____
_____
_____
_____

Have you been holding yourself back in any way? _____

_____
_____
_____
_____
_____
_____

What obstacles get in the way of your happiness?_____

What are your greatest gifts?_____

What are you holding back from your partner? Why is that?_____

What could you do to be happier? _____

_____

_____

_____

_____

_____

What are the positives about your role at home or at your job? __

_____

_____

_____

_____

_____

_____

What is it about your job or home life that cause stress? How can you address those? _____

_____

_____

_____

_____

_____

What is your biggest accomplishment as a person, partner, and parent? _____

_____

_____

_____

_____

_____

Do you feel comfortable to have a respectful voice and stand up for yourself? Explain. _____

_____

_____

_____

_____

_____

Do you feel comfortable to be vulnerable? Explain. _____

_____

_____

_____

_____

_____

How are you feeling in your family life? _____

_____

_____

_____

_____

_____

Are there certain family members who drain your energy? _____

_____

_____

_____

_____

_____

Are you holding grudges against a family member? If so, why? What can you do to address these? _____

_____

_____

_____

_____

What are you thankful for about your relationships? i.e., family of origin, your partner, your children? _____

_____

_____

_____

_____

_____

How are you feeling at the present moment? Are you feeling distressed, disturbed, or worried about something? _____

_____

_____

_____

_____

Are you overthinking anything? What do you need to do to address these in a healthy way? _____

_____

_____

_____

_____

Does anything from the past still affect you? What can you do to let go of the past? _____

_____

_____

_____

_____

_____

What are the questions you are afraid of being asked? Explain.

_____

_____

_____

_____

_____

What are your worst fears? What could you do to manage them if they became true? _____

_____

_____

_____

_____

Are you really who you are? Or do the circumstances make you appear different? Explain. _____
_____
_____
_____
_____
_____
_____

What do you see when you look in the mirror? And what do you tell yourself about you?_____
_____
_____
_____
_____
_____

Are you disappointed in yourself? Is your reason(s) factual-based or feeling-based?_____
_____
_____
_____
_____
_____

What can you do to improve your mental health? _____

_____

_____

_____

_____

_____

_____

What does self-forgiveness mean to you? _____

_____

_____

_____

_____

_____

_____

Do you need to forgive yourself? Explain. _____

_____

_____

_____

_____

_____

Do you still have a hard time accepting the truth about your relationship, yourself, your partner and the betrayal? _____

_____
_____
_____
_____
_____

What do you love about your body? _____

_____
_____
_____
_____
_____

What is something you don't like about yourself? How can you change or embrace it? _____

_____
_____
_____
_____
_____

Are you taking care of your body and your overall physical health? If not, how can you start? _____

_____

_____

_____

_____

_____

Based on your answers, do you have better insight about your own mental and physical health? What do you need to do to improve your overall well-being? _____

_____

_____

_____

_____

What kind of relationship do you have with yourself? _____

_____

_____

_____

_____

Do you criticise yourself over every little mistake? Or do you talk to yourself in a supportive way?_____

_____

_____

_____

_____

Which relationships are the most important for you at the moment, and which one do you cherish the most?_____

_____

_____

_____

_____

Which relationships make you feel empty or distressed? What do you need to do?_____

_____

_____

_____

_____

Do you have a healthy relationship with your partner, your children? _____

_____

_____

_____

_____

Based on evidence, which relationships make you question your self-worth and affect your self-confidence, decision-making abilities, and guilt trip you? _____

_____

_____

_____

_____

_____

Who is the person in your life with whom you need to spend more time or less time? _____

_____

_____

_____

_____

Do you get angry and defensive when someone/partner disagrees with you? Explain. _____
_____
_____
_____
_____

At times, do you recognise control issues in your own behaviours? How can you address them? _____
_____
_____
_____
_____
_____
_____

Are you living your dream life? If not, what do you need to do to achieve those dreams? _____
_____
_____
_____
_____
_____

What kind of life do you want to live? Can you still create it? Explain. _____
_____
_____
_____
_____
_____
_____
_____
_____

What is your definition of success and relational happiness? ___
_____
_____
_____
_____
_____
_____
_____
_____

CHAPTER 9

What To Consider Before Ending Your Relationship

An unhealthy relationship deceives you into believing familiarity is security. Normalise your departure from a toxic partner because not everyone is relationship material.

Inability to replace the broken relational trust with ongoing safety.

You must initially look for safety, which is a process in your relationship if the foundation of relational trust has been destroyed by betrayal. Living an intimate and full life is possible when you feel safe. As a result of safety, intimacy and vulnerability (which is when you can express your truth) develop. However, you should only consider this alternative if your partner genuinely wants to change and demonstrates transformative change. How do you know if your partner who betrayed you is safe now? If the person who betrayed you does not express genuine remorse or show behavioural change, there is not much hope for safety. Pay attention and note if your partner's words and actions align on a consistent basis. If this is not the case, it is time to exit.

Does your partner exhibit a poor ability to recover?

It is time to leave if your partner is not making progress in their recovery, is not transparent, is continuing to be dishonest, shows no sign of remorse for their past betrayal, or still secretly relapses.

Are your relational and personal boundaries respected or violated?

It is time to really re-evaluate your relationship if you are still having trouble getting your boundaries respected or if they are being ignored in the name of incapability or a lack of understanding. If your boundaries for reconciliation following betrayal are still breached, you must present yourself with an exit plan.

If your mental health is affected.

Your well-being and general health can benefit from interactions that are healthy and positive. However, you might need to think about whether to end the relationship if it is unhealthy, unsafe, or no longer meaningful and enjoyable.

Consult a mental health professional.

Think about seeking mental health assistance and create your safety plans soon as you can. It could be helpful to talk about the end of a relationship before the intense associated emotions manifest.

Take into account everyone's overall physical safety.

Are any members of family—including you, your children, and others—currently in immediate danger? Take into account the safety and well-being of everyone involved as well as a safe location to remain during the separation procedure while deciding the best time to end the relationship.

Investigate your support network.

Take into account the people in your life that you can turn to for a variety of support. How can you get in touch with someone if you want to chat, need help with childcare, need accommodation or other types of support? Additionally, think about whether you should join a support group.

Discover any resources you might require.

If you can, try to save up enough money for at least a few months. Consider the additional resources you will need and how to get to them, such as childcare and legal services.

To protect your children's mental health, consider how and when to tell them.

Keep your children's best interests in mind when deciding how to tell them that your relationship is ending, who will obtain custody, and how to take care of their needs. Children should not be involved in adult issues. Please use child-appropriate language, maintain respect for your partner, and avoid attempting to sway the children's opinion when talking to them about your partner or the separation. To help your children cope with the separation, think about employing resources like therapists and school counsellors.

QUESTIONS

Following a betrayal, what behavioural adjustments in your partner signal relational safety?_____

_____

_____

What is your action plan in light of relational safety? Continue or end your relationship?_____

_____

_____

What are the adjustments you would like your partner to make that they haven't yet?_____

_____

_____

_____

What is your safety plan if you have to end your current relationship?_____

_____

_____

_____

How would you provide for your physical, financial, and emotional needs as well as those of your children, if you have any? _____

_____
_____
_____
_____

What are your motivations or plans if you are still in a toxic relationship? _____

_____
_____
_____
_____

What fears do you have about ending your toxic relationship? How can they be dealt with? _____

_____
_____
_____
_____

If you knew you could not fail, what would be your decision today? To remain or leave your relationship? _____

_____
_____
_____
_____

How would your life change if your partner suddenly passed away?
_____
_____
_____

If you did not care about your fears or other people's opinions, what type of life would you lead?_____
_____
_____
_____

What does co-dependency mean to you?_____
_____
_____
_____

Do you consider yourself to be in a co-dependent relationship? Explain._____
_____
_____
_____

What positive attributes about yourself did the betrayal highlight?
_____
_____
_____

CHAPTER 10

Step Zero And 12 Steps For Processing Your Betrayal Trauma

Some betrayed partners require and gain from thoroughly considered 12-Steps recovery work. The 12-Steps system is a terrific tool, but I do not think it is necessary for everyone's healing after betrayal. Only you can decide if it works for you. It is for this reason that I have developed a version of 12 Steps that honour both your journey and the 12-Steps framework's historical background.

Steps 1 through 12 have been created based on the traditional 12 Steps (SA, 2001), and modified to meet the needs of the betrayed partner. The quotations at the start of each Step are direct quotes from the 12-Step system.

Step Zero

Explore how and why to do healing beyond betrayal

In order to fully heal, it is crucial to express your emotions. Learning to be comfortable with uncomfortable emotions or triggers without running away from or ignoring them, is the main goal of my nominated step zero.

In the past, you might not have known what an uncomfortable feeling was if you experienced one. You might have thought the emotion would disappear if you stayed busy and ignored it. Effective healing, however, involves training your ability to identify and deal with your needs and uncomfortable feelings. For instance, you might be able to recognise the behaviour or actions that came before a trigger or a cycle of your partner's relapse. Avoid reactivity, and progress in your healing. You could struggle to identify and sit in your emotions immediately after learning about your partner's betrayal, during multi-layered and complex grief-processing, and when the trauma-brain is activated. Nevertheless, develop discipline and perform the feeling exercise (see below). Ideally daily. Keep in mind that your partner alone is entirely accountable for the betrayal they perpetrated, but only *you* are accountable for your own healing.

Being a victim is a sweet state to reside. There is no accountability to accept, and wallowing in self-pity eventually gets old. I am here to let you know that nobody is coming to heal or save you. You have to actively pursue it yourself.

Feeling Exercise

1. Notice, identify, and name all your feelings here and now.
   I feel...................... because............................
   For example: I feel resentful that my partner is not consistent in doing relational recovery work.

2. What is each feeling trying to communicate to you?
   For example: Resentfulness is communicating to me that I am suppressing my emotions thus having this silent voice of anger eating me up.

3. What is your action plan to address them wholesomely?
   For example: My action plan is to start developing a respectful voice and express to my partner my boundaries, wants, and needs to feel safe.

4. How do you apply the lesson(s) from your identified emotions into your daily life?
   For example: I will be honest with my partner about how I really feel without criticising or placing blame on them. I will also let them know that we need to schedule a specific time to work on our recovery together in order to maintain the boundaries between us. I will start carrying this out right away.

5. Gratitude for what is going right in your life.
   For example: I am grateful that my partner and I are getting better in communication and trigger management.

QUESTIONS

Below, try and answer the "Why" questions:

Why did you choose to maintain or end your relationship with your partner who betrayed you?_____

_____

_____

_____

_____

Why is it necessary for you to heal, regardless of your relationship status?_____

_____

_____

_____

What are your healing goals, and how do you plan to achieve them?

_____

_____

_____

_____

Where are you in the process of healing? Why?_____

_____

_____

_____

_____

Step Zero And 12 Steps For Processing Your Betrayal Trauma

What aspects of recovery do you resist the most, and why?_____

_____

_____

_____

How might your ability to heal, or lack thereof, affect your relationships and general quality of life?_____

_____

_____

_____

Why would it be appealing for some to continue to suffer and be a victim?_____

_____

_____

_____

Are you prepared to get past the pain and victimisation the betrayal caused? Why now?_____

_____

_____

_____

What benefits would you receive from completing the following 12 Steps?_____

_____

_____

Step 1

"We admitted that we were powerless over our partner's sexual addiction and that our lives had become unmanageable."

Explore your "powerlessness" over your partner's condition and recovery

To take the first step and admit your powerlessness over your partner's sexual addiction, you must first understand and accept that sexual addiction is a mind-altering disease. This is a chronic addiction that cannot be cured, just controlled, very much like addiction to drugs and alcohol. You must learn to maintain your focus on yourself in order to heal. As you reflect on the past betrayal, you are urged to acknowledge your powerlessness over the betrayal, the sexual addiction, and your partner's addiction. In doing so, a great burden is removed, and you start to see the freedom and power you actually do possess.

Additionally, anxiety decreases when you let go of the false sense of control over other people, their behaviour, and the events. You become more focused and start to see the paths to your own healing. You eventually pick up new techniques for maintaining wholesome relationships in every aspect of your life. Step one gets you in the right relationship with yourself because when you try to control your partner, their recovery, or other people, you lose control over your own life. Give up control. Remember, you have no control if your partner decides to get sober or they relapse. Nobody but yourself is under your control.

QUESTIONS

What does being powerless mean to you in relation to the betrayal?

_____
_____
_____
_____

How difficult is it to accept that your partner has betrayed you?

_____
_____
_____
_____

What aspects of the betrayal were under your control?_____

_____
_____
_____
_____

Who (you or your partner) is powerless over their actions, and why? Explain._____

_____
_____
_____
_____

What does it mean to you to acknowledge your powerlessness in the face of your partner's possible relapse?_____
_____
_____
_____

What distinguishes your powerlessness over your partner's addiction from their powerlessness over their own addiction?___
_____
_____
_____
_____

Admit that your partner's sex addiction was caused by you or not. Explain._____
_____
_____
_____
_____

In light of your admittance that you have no power over your partner's recovery going forward, what is your action plan?_____
_____
_____
_____
_____

What aspects of your partner's recovery are under your direct control? _____

_____

_____

_____

What other areas of your life do you find yourself powerless? ___

_____

_____

_____

In what areas of your life do you have power? _____

_____

_____

_____

Whom do you have the power to change? You or your partner?

_____

_____

_____

_____

Could your partner's behaviour change as a result of your positive behaviour changes? Give one example. _____

_____

Are you prepared to make some positive behavioural changes in yourself for the sake of your relationship? Why now?_____

_____

_____

_____

If faith/spirituality is part of your life, how can God or a higher power help you let go of your control of the uncontrollable?____

_____

_____

_____

Write a letter to God or a higher power outlining the aspects of your past traumatic events that you had control over but failed to handle (such as your early years and your current relationship with the person who betrayed you)._____

_____

_____

_____

What does God/the higher power say in response to the letter?

_____

_____

_____

Step 2

"We came to believe that a power greater than ourselves could restore us to sanity."

Explore Your Spirituality And Identify Your True God/Higher Power

It is incredibly healing to come to trust in a single force that can support you and guide you through this trying process. Through the potent gift of other people—hearing them, seeing them, and witnessing the gift of recovery at work in their lives—you can begin to believe in a better life and a higher power. A true hope that you have an essence and a purpose, that things will improve and have an impact on you and your life, comes from thinking that a power greater than you exists. It does not resemble a "DIY program" for your recovery when you connect to God or a higher power. In this space, you develop the belief that there is a force greater than yourself that will help you achieve your goals in life since even your most devoted efforts will fall short of what this force can do for you. God/your higher power will bring you back to a sensible and prosperous existence. All that is required is faith.

Seek, observe, be curious, and bear witness to others and notice the comfort they have found. Discover your personal faith, belief, and journey. Open your heart to your higher power and start praying even if you do not believe.

QUESTIONS

How do you currently perceive spirituality, God, or a higher power?
_____
_____
_____
_____

Has your belief in God or a higher power changed as a result of prior experiences? If so, how?_____
_____
_____
_____

What advantages might your spirituality offer you as you heal or recover?_____
_____
_____

Do you need to pray? Explain._____
_____
_____

How beneficial to your overall recovery/healing would prayer/meditation be?_____
_____
_____

Without relying on God or a higher power, can you endure the grief caused by betrayal? Explain. _____

_____

_____

_____

Have you ever experienced any paranormal or spiritual encounters that suggested God or another higher power might be real? ____

_____

_____

_____

Write a letter to God or a higher power in which you freely express your true feelings towards your partner who betrayed you. _____

_____

_____

_____

How would God or a higher power answer your previous letter?

_____

_____

_____

_____

Step 3

"We made a decision to turn our will and our lives over to the care of God as we understood Him."

Explore How To Relinquish Control Over The Uncontrollable And Ask God Or A Higher Power To Provide You With The Courage And Knowledge To Do So

Spending time intentionally with God and learning about His existence and the nature of this connection constitutes step two. This is a way that God or a higher power acts in your favour because you believe in and want to be connected to Him. Making a decision of this significance can and should take some time during your recovery journey. Giving your life to God is comparable to making a lifelong commitment to a long-term partner. This relationship grows with time. Your understanding of God will increase as a result of your personal and shared experiences.

QUESTIONS

What do you think about seeking guidance from God or a higher power?

How can you discover your higher power, and who or what it may be?

Are you prepared to surrender your problems? What might make you more willing?

How can you decide to give yourself over to God or a higher power without delaying any longer?

Is your concept of a higher power a helpful one? Explain. _____

_____

_____

_____

_____

What will occur if you decide not to establish or re-establish your connection with and surrender to God/higher power? _____

_____

_____

_____

_____

What advantages would there be in asking God or a higher authority for help or guidance? _____

_____

_____

_____

_____

What help or guidance, if you believe in God or a higher power, would you request? _____

_____

_____

_____

_____

Step 4

"We made a searching and fearless moral inventory of ourselves."

Explore And Acknowledge Your Own Shortcomings And Personality Flaws

Making an assessment of yourself is advantageous in many ways, although many betrayed partners do not like this step. An inventory first tells you what happened and when it happened. Additionally, this collection will assist you in comprehending your unhealthy behaviour cycles or patterns. A fourth step can be done in a number of ways, but they all require writing them down. Step four is where you discover the truth of who you are. With the aid of this moral inventory, you can move forward in your process of grief and healing. You will never stop being a victim if you keep blaming others for your problems, but if you genuinely look at your own behaviours, viewpoints, and attitudes, you will discover that a large portion of your suffering is brought on and controllable by you.

The most crucial realisation is that hiding your flaws and being ashamed of them are manifestations of pride and ego, of which you need to let go. Keep in mind that you are the key to whatever change you want to see because you are the only person you can change and control.

QUESTIONS

Make a list of all your character flaws? _____

_____

_____

_____

_____

List the instances in which each of your character flaws appears?

_____

_____

_____

_____

_____

_____

What effects do your personality flaws have on the various people in your life? _____

_____

_____

_____

_____

List the steps you will take to address each character flaw if it resurfaces in the future.

What are some of your character flaws that could hamper your progress to effective healing?

Can you identify resentment, fear, judgemental attitude, righteousness, self-pity, shame or avoidance behaviours? When and why and how are these activated?

List your positive attributes. _____
_____
_____
_____
_____

How could your positive attributes aid your healing/recovery? __
_____
_____
_____
_____

What ways do your character flaws impair your positive attributes?
_____
_____
_____
_____

How has working through step four impacted you? _____
_____
_____
_____
_____

Step 5

"We admitted to God, to ourselves, and to another human being the exact nature of our wrongs."

Explore Admitting Your Shortcomings To God/Higher Power And Your Safe People

You identified your shortcomings and gave yourself the information you needed to perform steps four and five. "Admitting to God" has been a profound and therapeutic experience for some betrayed partners. Recounting your story to God or a higher power and confessing it brings about healing. Step five involves reading God your inventory from step four while praying or visualising yourself in His presence. The hardest thing is, without a doubt, admitting to "another human being". Although it may be challenging, allowing someone else in is absolutely essential for your restoration. Complete this step first and foremost with your therapist or another trusted person. A carefully selected third party such as your therapist will point out any areas where you have not been completely sincere in your efforts to right your wrongs. Therefore, to the best of your abilities, you must be honest with this person and admit all of your flaws.

QUESTIONS

Why must you confess your flaws in detail to another person as opposed to just yourself and God? _____
_____
_____
_____
_____
_____
_____

How does confessing your flaws to another safe person help you heal? _____
_____
_____
_____
_____
_____
_____
_____

Write a letter to God/higher power and admit all your shortcomings and also share step five with your therapist and, if you wish, another safe person. _____

_____

_____

_____

_____

_____

_____

_____

_____

List some of your shortcomings in the form of unhelpful beliefs that you still carry from your childhood into your adult relationships._____

_____

_____

_____

_____

_____

How much of your sexual freedom after experiencing betrayal trauma is impacted by your early-life negative experiences or your current unhelpful beliefs?_____
_____
_____
_____
_____
_____
_____
_____

What is your action plan to address every distorted belief about yourself?_____
_____
_____
_____
_____
_____
_____
_____
_____

What are some favourable traits that people might have about you?

What are some positive beliefs you hold about yourself?

Step Six

"We were entirely ready to have God remove all these defects of character."

Explore How With God's/Higher Power's Help You Can Replace Your Shortcomings With Your Positive Attributes

The sixth step is an inspirational goal to surrender to your god/higher power's guidance. By finishing step six, you will be able to take one day at a time and let go of all the unhealthy survival techniques you have been using in favour of more healthy ones. For instance, excessively attending to your anxieties allowed you to keep up the impression that you were in control. The reality is that you still have no control over anything that has happened in the past, will happen in the future, or over many other things right now. However, your shortcomings became unhelpful survival tools and gave you the impression that you were in power because you were fearful of being powerless. A paradigm shift in and of itself occurs when one believes that God or a higher power is love. You take a step back and declare that you are willing to change any attitude, thought pattern, or behavioural issues when you acknowledge that everything is part of God/higher power's design to love you in every facet of life.

When you awaken the next seven days, do the following:

Take a moment to acknowledge your feelings. Right before we begin the main activity of the day, we are frequently most vulnerable. Think about how you are feeling. Express your feelings to God/higher power in a few sentences. Commit to acknowledging, naming, and addressing your feelings. As soon as you can, express your feelings to a friend or write them down in a notebook before talking to a therapist about them. At any time throughout the day, repeat this exercise once more. Ideally, do it in the evening or right after dinner, or when the workday is over.

The next time a strong emotion comes over you—pain, fear, desire to control, anger, joy, blessedness, or gratitude—accept it, validate it, and sit in it. Later, after writing about it in a journal, call a friend and express it. Admit the emotion to God/higher power as soon as you can, and if it is negative, ask Him/them to take it away and replace it with a desirable thought, feeling, or behaviour. If it is positive, merely express gratitude and thanks for it.

QUESTIONS

What dysfunctional habits or coping strategies do you need to let go of? For example: excessive drinking, shopping, working, or screen time. Other avoidance, dysfunctional or escaping behaviours? _____

_____

_____

_____

_____

Do any of these patterns apply to you? How? What would you use to replace each? _____

_____

_____

_____

Co-dependency? How? _____

_____

_____

_____

Replace with:_____

_____

_____

Controlling behaviours? How?_____

_____

_____

_____

Replace with:_____

_____

_____

_____

Manipulation? How? _____

_____

_____

_____

Replace with:_____

_____

_____

_____

Fears and anxiety? How?_____
_____
_____
_____

Replace with:_____
_____
_____
_____
_____

Negative, limiting beliefs? How?_____
_____
_____
_____
_____

Replace with:_____
_____
_____
_____
_____

Stuck in the past? How?_____
_____
_____
_____

Replace with:_____

_____

_____

_____

Being a victim and needing to place the blame for your pain on others? How?_____

_____

_____

_____

Replace with:_____

_____

_____

_____

Putting off living and awaiting the ideal circumstances for happiness? How?_____

_____

_____

_____

Replace with:_____

_____

_____

_____

Self-esteem? How?_____
_____
_____
_____

Replace with:_____
_____
_____

Self-neglect and lack of self-care, and the conviction you are not accountable to or capable of caring for yourself? How?_____
_____
_____
_____

Replace with:_____
_____
_____

Your desire to have to wait for others to make you happy? How?
_____
_____

Replace with:_____
_____
_____

Self-rejection? How?_____

_____

_____

_____

Replace with:_____

_____

_____

Self-hatred? How?_____

_____

_____

_____

Replace with:_____

_____

_____

_____

Lack of self-trust? How?_____

_____

_____

_____

Replace with:_____

_____

_____

Lack of trust in God/higher power, life, and the process of recovery? How?_____
_____
_____
_____

Replace with:_____
_____
_____
_____

Poor personal and relational boundaries? How?_____
_____
_____
_____

Replace with:_____
_____
_____
_____

Poor body image?_____
_____
_____

Replace with:_____
_____
_____

Which behaviours that you previously relied on to help you, now hinder your progress?_____

_____
_____
_____
_____

Is there something going on that you need to talk about but do not want to? A need, a feeling, or an issue?_____

_____
_____
_____
_____

Do you currently need to talk to someone in your life but are attempting to postpone doing so because you are afraid to say something uncomfortable? Explain._____

_____
_____
_____
_____

Have you been unkind to yourself or someone else recently? Tell your therapist, a different trustworthy person, and God/higher power what you did._____

_____

_____

_____

_____

Has your pain led you to be willing to let go and let God/higher power take control? What does this mean? What does that look like?_____

_____

_____

_____

Which aspects of your character flaws have caused you to become isolated?_____

_____

_____

_____

_____

_____

Step 7

"We humbly asked Him to remove our shortcomings."

Explore What Humility Means To You And How It Can Counteract Your Personal Flaws

The first word in step seven—humbly—is the key since true humility can only be taught through failure. Humility comes easily when you are genuinely grateful to God or your higher power for giving you the capacity to move past setbacks and shortcomings. Humility and respect for oneself and others goes hand-in-hand. A humble person cherishes their own and other people's respect, in addition to being modest. The humble person does not condemn or judge their own failures and is tolerant of others' flaws. You learn to reflect on yourself, become more self-aware, and develop tolerance for others and for yourself when you are humble.

It is a difficult spiritual discipline to ask God/higher power to remove your flaws, eliminate your ego, and grant you humility. You could find it helpful to jot down a paragraph or two explaining how your ego or lack of humility has worsened your personal shortcomings and have hurt both yourself and others as a result. Just make an effort to recognise two flaws in yourself every day, along with how ego has preserved those flaws and how integrating humility will correct them.

QUESTIONS

How do you define humility? _____
_____
_____
_____
_____

Where in your journey do you identify you ego hampering your progress? _____
_____
_____
_____
_____

Identify five of your personal flaws and how lack of humility has preserved them. _____
_____
_____
_____
_____

How has your ego served you in the past and in the present?_____

_____
_____
_____
_____

Why would you want a higher power or God to make you humble and take away your ego?_____

_____
_____
_____

What do you fear about letting go of your ego? Are your fears based in fact or feelings?_____

_____
_____
_____

Give some examples of your humility and lack of ego that you have already noticed in yourself. _____

_____
_____
_____

What kind of improvements are possible this week if you learn to be more humble? Explain.

Who are the three most crucial people with whom you should exercise humility?

What benefit would you personally get if you let go of your ego and adopted humility instead?

Have you noticed a shift in your connection to your god or higher power as you have completed step seven?

Step 8

"We made a list of all people we had harmed, and became willing to make amends to them all."

Explore Who You Need To Make Amends To, And Why

The eighth step is a simple one that entails journaling. Make a list of everyone you think you might have offended, and next to each name, state the reasons you think you may have harmed them. Read the list several times, as the goal of this step is to prepare you to be willing to admit and make amends. By defining your role in this step, you assume responsibility for your actions and free yourself from the burden of unwarranted responsibilities.

For instance, make a list of everyone you have insulted, using the example below.

I need to ask for forgiveness of *(name of the person)*_____
_____

because I did *(harmful behaviour)*_____
_____.

QUESTIONS

Make a list of the people you believe you have harmed. _____

_____
_____
_____
_____

Have you hurt the person that has betrayed you? Do they need to be on your list? If so, why?_____

_____
_____
_____
_____
_____

What are the challenges you have identified in making your list in step eight?_____

_____
_____
_____
_____
_____

Who are the people you hesitate to include on your list despite having harmed them? Explain. _____

_____
_____
_____
_____
_____

What have been the most effective means of amendments to the different persons you have wronged? _____

_____
_____
_____
_____
_____

What were the benefits of compiling your list in step eight? ____

_____
_____
_____
_____
_____

Step 9

"We made direct amends to such people wherever possible, except when to do so would injure them or others."

Explore Your Options For Delivering Your Amends To The People You Have Offended

In step nine, it is taken into account who your direct amends "may" distress. Making apologies to someone is a requirement of this step, and it cannot be avoided. Consult a therapist or someone who has finished step nine for advice if you think you are in such a situation. If they agree with you, you should generally skip making direct reparations in this situation. Writing next to each name on your list is the most direct method of making amends—in person, via phone, or in writing—and a very straightforward next step.

Consider composing a letter to someone who would be hurt by a direct amendment, but you will not necessarily send it to them. Instead, you will read it and process it with your therapist and another trustworthy person. You are ready to begin when your list of individuals and strategies is complete. To stay motivated to finish the entire list, it can be beneficial to record the dates you finished each amend.

QUESTIONS

List the individuals you have hurt, along with details on how you have hurt them. (Use the list from the previous steps.) _____

_____
_____
_____
_____
_____

Write the direct or indirect amends-methods for each person. __

_____
_____
_____
_____
_____
_____
_____
_____
_____
_____
_____

Did you have any amends to make with yourself? Explain._____
_____
_____
_____
_____

Discuss with a therapist or trustworthy person the reflections on the people to whom you have made amends._____
_____
_____
_____
_____

When are you completing your list?_____
_____
_____
_____
_____

What obstacles did you have to overcome to complete this step?
_____
_____
_____
_____
_____

What are the benefits of this step? _____

_____

_____

_____

_____

What does making amends mean? Does it mean reconciliation? Explain. _____

_____

_____

_____

_____

For whom did you make these amends? _____

_____

_____

_____

_____

Has your spirituality aided or hindered this process? _____

_____

_____

_____

_____

Step Ten

"We continued to take personal inventory, and when we were wrong, promptly admitted it."

Explore If You Are Practising The Steps Or Only Preaching Them

You have finished step nine by getting here, so congrats! The maintenance stage of the twelve steps is where you are currently. Step ten forbids you from harbouring any secrets or shame in your life after devoting time and energy to remove them. Making amends entails modifying one's behaviour as well as expressing regret for the offence. Arriving here indicates initiative, and every small step you take will be the beginning of something great.

Maintaining recovery calls for discipline. Journaling as a daily, personal inventory is the method you will employ in this phase to ensure that you are staying honest with both yourself and others. In this step, you will examine your daily actions to see if there was anything that you know to have been dishonest, egotistical, or harmful to you or others. Make amends if you need, whether it is to yourself or to someone else. This strategy, when fully integrated, can offer a lifestyle of humility and honesty for your own well-being and integrity with others. Keep in mind that making amends does not equal reconciliation.

QUESTIONS

Have you seen any improvements in yourself since completing the previous step? Explain.____

____

____

____

____

____

How do you create regular time and space to keep reflective journals? How significant is this ritual?____

____

____

____

____

Who was the last person you made amends with recently? Explain.

____

____

____

____

____

What is your process to make sure you are practising the steps instead of simply preaching them? _____
_____
_____
_____
_____
_____

Which of your current relationships is causing you the greatest distress? How would you address these issues? _____
_____
_____
_____
_____
_____

What steps must you take to look after your needs in your current unhealthy relationships? _____
_____
_____
_____
_____
_____

What would you say if you could be completely open and honest with one individual about your actions, your emotions, and your wants and needs? _____

_____

_____

_____

_____

What is your current major guilt? What approach would you take to address it? When would you make that approach? _____

_____

_____

_____

_____

Make amends for your self-harming thoughts, feelings, and actions by writing a letter to yourself. _____

_____

_____

_____

_____

In a letter to God or a higher power, state your intentions for learning to love and accept yourself.

Step 11

"We sought through prayer and meditation to improve our conscious contact with God as we understood Him, praying only for knowledge of His will for us and the power to carry that out."

Explore Your Conscious Relationship And Connection With God/Higher Power Through Prayer

The purpose of step eleven is to improve your communication and spiritual connection. You pray more regularly and deliberately throughout this stage to improve your conscious contact with the source. Feel free to express any thoughts you wish in your prayers to God/higher power, including requests, apologies, grievances, concerns, complaints, and other thoughts.

Praying is like talking to God/higher power knowing there is no judgement but total freedom to come as you are. Like the comfort of prayer, meditation helps you get deeper spiritually. There are significant goals for both prayer and meditation in this phase. Since you have managed to get to this step, you already have a connection to God/higher power. You now have the opportunity to further develop or strengthen that connection. Step eleven could lead you to a new spiritual dimension where you experience love, acceptance, and support, all of which could help you heal.

QUESTIONS

How often do you pray?_____
_____
_____
_____

Describe your favourite prayer using one example._____
_____
_____
_____

Do you hear what God/higher power tells you? Give an example.
_____
_____
_____
_____

What aspects of prayer and meditation are similar?_____
_____
_____
_____

How often do you meditate? _____

_____

_____

_____

What advantages have you experienced from praying and/or meditation? _____

_____

_____

_____

Have prayer or practising meditation led you to have a spiritual experience? If so, explain. _____

_____

_____

_____

_____

_____

_____

_____

Are you interested in deepening your spirituality? Explain.

What prevents you from advancing spiritually?

What are your rituals to reconnect with yourself?

Without a spiritual connection, is it possible to heal efficiently? Explain.

Write a letter to yourself from God/higher power outlining your purpose.

_____
_____
_____
_____
_____
_____
_____
_____

Write a letter to God/higher power expressing your understanding of your true purpose in the world.

_____
_____
_____
_____
_____
_____
_____
_____

Step 12

"Having had a spiritual awakening as the result of these steps, we tried to carry this message to others, and to practise these principles in all our affairs."

Explore Your Spiritual Connection And Consider The Best Way To Help Yourself And Other Betrayed Partners Learn From Your Valuable Experiences

Your whole journey could be summarised in step twelve, which reflects on the need for an ongoing spiritual awakening and connection, as well as sharing the testimonies and learnings with other betrayed partners.

The spiritual awakening is the first of several components in step twelve. A subjective experience known as spiritual awakening, which is a progressive process, occurs when a person's ego expands beyond their typical, limited sense of self to include a larger, infinite sense of truth or reality. Additionally, spiritual awakening can be defined as a strong sense of inner evolution, a profound awareness of the nature of existence, or a strong connection to the creator of the universe. It can promote a sense of harmony and unity as well as a deeper comprehension of one's purpose in life; a process of self-discovery and an opportunity to understand the universal spiritual truths.

Taking the lessons learned, applying them in daily life and also sharing them with other betrayed partners (who are safe and have boundaries) is another component in step twelve. Sharing your experiences and lessons must take place in safe settings and around safe people. These might include peer support groups, group therapy sessions, or betrayed partner groups. The most essential thing about this step is that it serves as a reminder that you have a responsibility to reach out and keep in touch. Keep in mind that hurt grows in isolation and that healing can only occur in connections and the comfort of a community.

Applying and practising all steps in daily life and whenever necessary, as opposed to saving them for therapy sessions or meetings, is the last component of step twelve.

A Summary Of The Principles Of 12 Steps For Betrayed Partners Are As Follows:

1. Honesty.
2. Hope.
3. Faith/action.
4. Courage.
5. Integrity.
6. Willingness.
7. Humility.
8. Brotherly/sisterly love.
9. Discipline/justice.
10. Perseverance.
11. Spiritual awareness.
12. Service.

QUESTIONS

How do you define spiritual awakening?

Have you experienced a spiritual awakening? Explain.

What would you gain from a spiritual awakening in terms of your healing?

How would you be able to tell if you were experiencing a spiritual awakening?_____

_____

_____

_____

What are some valuable lessons you have learned from this spiritual experience that you would like to share to others (both to sex addicts and betrayed partners)?_____

_____

_____

_____

_____

Do you reach out to others or your therapist when the need arises? Explain._____

_____

_____

_____

_____

What are different ways you could share your learnings with others?____

How can you share your wisdom to family members, even the ones who are the most resistant?____

How are you going to practise all learned principles in your daily life?____

What aspects of your life require additional consideration and the use of the 12 principles?_____

_____

_____

_____

_____

_____

Reflecting on your journey of healing and grief processing, where are you now?_____

_____

_____

_____

_____

What three lessons about yourself have you learned from this experience? Please share them._____

_____

_____

_____

_____

_____

_____

Who has been the hardest for you to get along with throughout this journey, and why?

"Then Jesus said, 'Come to me, all of you who are weary and carry heavy burdens, and I will give you rest. Take my yoke upon you. Let me teach you, because I am humble and gentle at heart, and you will find rest for your souls.'"

Matthew 11:28-29 NLT

References

American Psychological Association, (2022). *Control anger before it controls you*. https://www.apa.org/topics/anger/control

American Psychological Association, (2022a). *APA Dictionary of Psychology*. Apa.org. https://dictionary.apa.org/bargaining stage

American Psychological Association, (2022b). *APA Dictionary of Psychology*. Apa.org. https://dictionary.apa.org/stages-of-grief

American Psychiatric Association. (2022). *Diagnostic And Statistical Manual Of Mental Disorders*, Fifth Edition, Text Revision (5th ed.). American Psychiatric Association Publishing.

Azizi, M. R., & Vaezzadeh, A. (2021). A Study of External Music in Divan-e-Hafiz be-Al-Arabiyyate She'ran Translated by Nader Nezam Tehrani (Based on the first twenty Ghazals). *Translation Researches in the Arabic Language And Literature*, 11(25), 9-31.

Barker, M., Brewer, R., and Murphy, J. (2021). What is Interoception and Why is it Important?. *Frontiers for Young Minds*. 9:558246. https://doi.org/10.3389/frym.2021.558246

Bonanno, G.A., Malgaroli, M. (2019). Trajectories of grief: Comparing symptoms from the DSM-5 and ICD-11 diagnoses. *Depression and Anxiety*. https://doi.org/10.1002/da.22902

Bonanno, G. A., & Kaltman, S. (2001). The varieties of grief experience. *Clinical Psychology Review*, 21(5), 705–734.

Bugen, L. A. (1977). Human grief: A model for prediction and intervention. *American Journal of Orthopsychiatry*, 47(2), 196–206. https://doi.org/10.1111/j.1939-0025.1977.tb00975.x

Charteris, J., Page, A., Anderson, J., & Tomkinson, E. (2020).

What is relational trust and how do we foster it in our schools?. *Good Teacher Magazine*. University of New England. https://hdl.handle.net/1959.11/28658

Chatmon, B. N. (2020). Males and Mental Health Stigma. *American Journal of Men's Health*, 14(4). https://doi: 10.1177/1557988320949322. PMID: 32812501; PMCID: PMC7444121.

Courtois, C. A. (2009). *Understanding complex trauma, complex reactions, and treatment approaches*. Christine A. Courtois, PhD and Associates, PLC, Washington, DC. Available at: http://www.aaets.org/traumatic-stress-library/understanding-complex-trauma-complex-reactions-and-treatment-approaches

Craig, A. D. (2002). How do you feel? Interoception: the sense of the physiological condition of the body. *Nature Reviews Neuroscience*, 3(8), 655–666. https://doi: 10.1038/nrn894

Enright, R., & Human Development Study Group. (1996). Counseling within the for forgiveness triad: On forgiving, receiving forgiveness and self-forgiveness. *Counseling and Values*, 40(2), 107-126. https://doi.org/10.1002/j.2161-007X.1996.tb00844.x

Fisher, M., & Axline, J. J. (2006). Self-forgiveness versus excusing: The roles of remorse, effort, and acceptance of responsibility, *Self and Identity*, 5(2), 127-146. https://doi.org/10.1080/15298860600586123

Friedman, R., & James, J. W. (2009). The myth of the stages of dying, death and grief. *Counseling Today*, 51(9), 48–50.

Freyd, J. J. (2008). *The Encyclopedia of Psychological Trauma* (G. Reyes, J. D. Elhai, & J. D. Ford, Eds.). John Wiley & Sons, Inc.

Freyd, J. J. (1997). II. Violations of power, adaptive blindness and betrayal trauma theory. *Feminism & Psychology*, 7(1), 22-32.

Freyd, J. J. (2020). *What is a Betrayal Trauma? What is Betrayal*

Trauma Theory? Retrieved from https://dynamic.uoregon.edu/jjf/defineBT.html

Freyd, J. J., & Birrell, P. J. (2013). Blind to Betrayal: *Why We Fool Ourselves We Aren't Being Fooled.* John Wiley & Sons, Inc.

Friedman, R. A. (2012). Grief, depression, and the DSM-5. *The New England Journal of Medicine.*

Glass, S. (2007). *Not just friends: Rebuilding trust and recovering your sanity after infidelity.* Simon & Schuster.

Glass, S.P. (2004). *Not just friends: Rebuilding trust and recovering your sanity.* New York: Simon & Schuster.

Goldsmith, R. E., Freyd, J. J., & DePrince, A. P. (2012). Betrayal Trauma: Associations With Psychological and Physical Symptoms in Young Adults. *Journal of Interpersonal Violence*, 27(3), 547-567. https://doi.org/10.1177/0886260511421672

Gotink, R. A., Meijboom, R., Vernooij, M. W., Smits, M., & Hunink, M. M. (2016). 8-week mindfulness based stress reduction induces brain changes similar to traditional long-term meditation practice–a systematic review. *Brain and cognition*, 108, 32-41.

Gottman, J. (1995). *Why Marriages Succeed or Fail: And How You Can Make Yours Last.* Simon & Schuster.

Gottman, J. M. (2011). *The science of trust: Emotional attunement for couples.* W. W. Norton & Company.

Gottman, J., & Gottman, J. (2017a). The Natural Principles of Love. *Journal of Family Theory and Review*, 9(1), 7–26. https://doi.org/10.1111/JFTR.12182

Gottman, J., & Gottman, J. (2017b). *Treating Affairs and Trauma.* Unpublished manuscript, Gottman Institute, Seattle, USA.

Gottman, J. M., & Levenson, R. W. (1986). Assessing the role of emotion in marriage. *Behavioral Assessment*.

Gottman, J. M., & Levenson, R. W. (1992). Marital processes predictive of later dissolution: behavior, physiology, and health. *Journal of Personality and Social Psychology*, 63(2), 221–233. https://doi.org/10.1037/0022-3514.63.2.221

Gottman, J. M., & Levenson, R. W. (2002). A Two-Factor Model for Predicting When a Couple Will Divorce: Exploratory Analyses Using 14-Year Longitudinal Data. *Family Process*, 41(1), 83–96. https://doi.org/10.1111/J.1545-5300.2002.40102000083.X

Goyal, M., Singh, S., Sibinga, E. M., Gould, N. F., Rowland-Seymour, A., Sharma, R., ... & Haythornthwaite, J. A. (2014). Meditation programs for psychological stress and well-being: a systematic review and meta-analysis. *JAMA internal medicine*, 174(3), 357-368.

Gupta, S. (2022). *What to Know About the Acceptance Stage of Grief*. https://www.verywellmind.com/the-acceptance-stage-of-grief-characteristics-and-coping-5295854

Hall, C. (2011). Beyond Kübler-Ross: recent developments in our understanding of grief and bereavement. *InPsych: The Bulletin of the Australian Psychological Society Ltd*, 33(6), 8.

Holland, K. (2018). *What You Should Know About the Stages of Grief*. Retrieved from https://www.healthline.com/health/stages-of-grief

Hölzel BK, Carmody J, Vangel M, Congleton C, Yerramsetti SM, Gard T, Lazar SW. *Mindfulness practice leads to increases in regional brain gray matter density*. Psychiatry Res. 2011 Jan 30;191(1):36-43. https://doi.org/10.1016/j.pscychresns.2010.08.006. Epub 2010 Nov 10. PMID: 21071182; PMCID: PMC3004979.

Khalsa, S. S., Adolphs, R., Cameron, O. G., Critchley, H. D.,

Davenport, P. W., Feinstein, J. S., et al. (2018). Interoception and mental health: a roadmap. *Biological Psychiatry Cognitive Neuroscience*. Neuroimaging 3:501–13. https://doi.org/10.1016/j.bpsc.2017.12.004

Klass, D., Nickman, L.N., Silverman, P.R. (1996). Continuing Bonds: *New Understandings of Grief (Death Education, Aging and Health Care)*. New York: Routledge.

Kleinert T, Schiller B, Fischbacher U, et al. (2020). *The Trust Game for Couples (TGC): A new standardized paradigm to assess trust in romantic relationships*. PLoS One. 2020;15(3):e0230776. https://doi.org/10.1371/journal.pone.0230776

Konigsberg, R. D. (2011). *The truth about grief: The myth of its five stages and the new science of loss*. Simon & Schuster.

Kübler-Ross, E., & Kessler, D. (2014). *On grief & grieving: Finding the meaning of grief through the five stages of loss* (Scribner trade pbk. ed.). Scribner.

Kübler-Ross, E. (1969). *On death and dying*. New York: MacMillan.

Kübler-Ross, E. (2009). *On death and dying: What the dying have to teach doctors, nurses, clergy and their own families*. Taylor & Francis.

Kübler-Ross, E. (1970). *On death and dying*. Macmillan.

Liddon, L., Kingerlee, R., Barry. J. A. Gender differences in preferences for psychological treatment, coping strategies, and triggers to help-seeking. Br J Clin Psychol. 2018 Mar;57(1):42-58. https://doi.org/10.1111/bjc.12147. Epub 2017 Jul 9. PMID: 28691375.

Lilienfeld, S. O., Lynn, S. J., Ruscio, J., & Beyerstein, B. L. (2010). Busting big myths in popular psychology. *Scientific American Mind*, 21(1), 42–49.

Lotterman, J. H., Bonanno, G. A., & Galatzer-Levy, I. (2014).

The heterogeneity of long-term grief reactions. *Journal of Affective Disorders*, 167, 12–19. https://doi.org.libproxy.unm.edu/10.1016/j.jad.2014.05.048

Lusterman, D. (1998). Infidelity: A survival guide. California USA: New Harbinger Publications Inc.

Möller glue cooler, AM (2009). Men, depression and male depression. *Advances in Neurology · Psychiatry*, 77 (07), 412-422.

Mrazek, M. D., Franklin, M. S., Phillips, D. T., Baird, B., & Schooler, J. W. (2013). Mindfulness training improves working memory capacity and GRE performance while reducing mind wandering. *Psychological science*, 24(5), 776-781.

Murphy, J., Catmur, C., and Bird, G. 2019. Classifying individual differences in interoception: implications for the measurement of interoceptive awareness. *Psychon. Bull. Rev.* 26:1467–71. https://doi.org/10.3758/s13423-019-01632-7

Murphy, J., Brewer, R., Catmur, C., and Bird, G. 2017. Interoception and psychopathology: a developmental neuroscience perspective. *Dev. Cogn. Neurosci.* 23:45–56. https://doi.org/10.1016/j.dcn.2016.12.006

Neimeyer, R. A. (2012). The (half) truth about grief. *Illness Crisis and Loss*, 20(4), 389–396.

O'Connor, M. F. (2019). Grief: A Brief History of Research on How Body, Mind, and Brain Adapt. *Psychosomatic Medicine*, 81(8), 731–738. https://doi.org/10.1097/psy.0000000000000717

Parent, M. C., Hammer, J. H., Bradstreet, T. C., Schwartz, E. N., & Jobe, T. (2018). Men's mental health help-seeking behaviors: An intersectional analysis. *American journal of men's health*, 12(1), 64-73.

Subotnik, R. & Harris, G. G. (1999). *Surviving infidelity: Making decisions, recovering from the pain*. (2nd ed). Toronto: Adams Media.

Van der Kolk, B. A. (2014). *The body keeps the score: Brain, mind, and body in the healing of trauma*. Viking.

Weller, F. (2015). *The wild edge of sorrow: Rituals of renewal and the sacred work of grief.* North Atlantic Books.

Werner, N. S., Jung, K., Duschek, S., and Schandry, R. 2009. Enhanced cardiac perception is associated with benefits in decision-making. *Psychophysiology* 46:1123–9. https://doi.org/10.1111/j.1469-8986.2009.00855.x

Worden, J. W. (1991). *Grief counselling and grief therapy: A handbook for the mental health practitioner (2nd edition)*. London: Springer.

About Author

Dr Fai Seyed lives in Brisbane, Australia, and has a PhD in sex addiction and its impact on female partners' well-being and lived experiences. In addition, she has a master's degree in counselling and psychotherapy, is a supervisor and trainer, and is a qualified oral and dental surgeon from Sweden. She has over 27 years of clinical experience in both public and private practice across Sweden, England, and Australia.

Dr Fai is an accomplished author of multiple books and academic articles on sex addiction and betrayal trauma in partners. Interacting with patients, friends, family members, staff, and other stakeholders who have struggled with sexual addiction has motivated her to progress in this field. Dr Seyed is working with sexual addicts and their partners and has designed a unique structured 12-week recovery and reconciliation framework.

Qualifications:

PhD, Master of counselling, Clinical counsellor/Supervisor SRT (Sexual Recovery therapist), Partners Betrayal Trauma therapy, Gottman (L1, L2), TRTP practitioner.

Neurofeedback provider, Sex addiction therapist, AASAT (American association of sex addiction therapy),

ACA level 3, CCAA reg. PACFA (Clinical)

Dental/Oral surgeon BDS, Sweden.

www.houseofhopecounselling.com.au

enquiries@houseofhopecounselling.com.au

Services and Offers

Sex addiction therapy for individuals and their partners (AASAT; American Association for Sex Addiction Therapy), AASAT Betrayal Partner Recovery Specialist, AASAT Intimacy Anorexia Specialist, Gottman (level 1, 2), NLP, Hypnosis, NeurOptimal® neurofeedback, EMDR, trauma and PTSD management, infidelity recovery, Gestalt therapy, cognitive behavioural therapy, mindfulness practise, betrayal trauma, ADHD, depression and family therapy.

Bonus for finishing this book:

30 minutes free consultation with Dr Fai where you can have all your questions answered in private.

Contact details

Ph. 0413 482 486

www.houseofhopecounsellingcentre.com.au

enquiries@houseofhopecounselling.com.au

Other books by Dr Fai Seyed

www.ingramcontent.com/pod-product-compliance
Lightning Source LLC
Chambersburg PA
CBHW050307010526
44107CB00055B/2131